Fourth Edition

GROUP DISCUSSION

A Practical Guide to Participation and Leadership

Kathryn Sue Young
Julia T. Wood
Gerald M. Phillips
Douglas J. Pedersen

WAVELAND

PRESS, INC.

Long Grove, Illinois

For information about this book, contact:
Waveland Press, Inc.
4180 IL Route 83, Suite 101
Long Grove, IL 60047-9580
(847) 634-0081
info@waveland.com
www.waveland.com

🍂 Contents 🍂

11 Standard Agenda Step Five: Discovering and Selecting Solutions   **141**

12 Standard Agenda Step Six: Preparing and Presenting the Final Report   **153**

❧ Preface ❧

It has been over 20 years since this book was originally published, and while editions have changed, our goals remain the same: (1) to create an affordable and easy-to-read group communication textbook and (2) to provide a specific problem-solving agenda that is applicable to any problem-solving discussion. This textbook differs from other group discussion texts in that we spend entire chapters outlining the steps of one problem-solving procedure, allowing you to learn problem-solving skills in great detail. If you will be working on a problem-solving project or you want to enhance your group discussion skills, this book is for you.

Kathryn Sue Young

FROM THE ORIGINAL AUTHORS

The main theme of this book is that collective action for problem solving must be systematic, for within a system is the greatest chance of displaying mutual respect and encouraging creativity. This book does not reflect a "paint by numbers" approach to problem solving. The authors have had more than fifty years of collective experience working with a great many types of groups in communities, education, industry, and government. Ours is a practical approach that recognizes the creative potential of the individual human and acknowledges that synergy between individual and group is the best way to realize that potential.

We hope to help people become effective participants and leaders in whatever groups they serve. We regard speaking in groups as a special form of rhetoric, a way for the individual to exert his or her influence, to work for the common good, and to enhance self-esteem by contributing to the welfare of all. Such a powerful system demands skill, experience, and knowledge. We offer the background and the instruction by which knowledge can inform performance, informed performance can become skill, and constant skillful behavior can become experience. The classroom professor and the students who use this book become the actors in the drama of learning to work together.

Julia T. Wood
Gerald M. Phillips
Douglas J. Pedersen

Acknowledgements

The fourth edition of this book is dedicated in loving memory of Gerald M. Phillips. He was an inspiration to his students and taught us about much more than speech communication during graduate school. I would also like to express my deepest gratitude to Julia Wood, Doug Pedersen, and Nancy Phillips who graciously allowed me to work on this project.

I am truly grateful to my business partner, Howard Travis, for his work editing my words and always being there to support me. I am appreciative of my colleague, Bia Bernum, who constantly helps me to come up with a new way of looking at things. As always, the editors at Waveland Press were fantastic to work with, and I thank them for their insight and ability to make the writing better. I continue to be indebted to Carol Rowe who is an inspiration in every step of the process. Without her support, I would have never written my first book. Thank you, Carol, for everything you do!

A number of students also made tremendous contributions and suggestions for this edition. The spring 2004 small group class gave the text an extensive critique and offered suggestions. Erica Hudock also helped me to complete much of the new research for this edition.

Finally, I would like to thank my husband, Joel, and my daughters, Laura, Samantha, and Claire, for their support and understanding as I worked on this project.

Kathryn Sue Young

✺ 1 ✺

Introduction to Group Discussion and the Standard Agenda

> The group members were frustrated. How could the semester be off to such a bad start? After all, this was only the second group meeting! Tanisha was so excited to share the group name and slogan she had developed, but the group seemed reluctant to approve the use of her ideas. Dan was upset because the group seemed unconcerned with setting up an operating structure. It was clear to him that nothing could be accomplished until they decided who was going to be the leader. Lorrie couldn't understand why the group didn't want to focus on the tasks; the instructor had just given them four project assignments that had to be completed soon. To her it made sense for them to prioritize tasks and to work on the most important first. How could Tanisha be so concerned with a group name when it wasn't needed for another couple of weeks?

How many times have you left group meetings feeling angry and dissatisfied? Unfortunately, people sometimes experience more negative effects when working with groups than positive ones. Why is this? We work with groups from the time we are in grade school, yet some adults continue to experience difficulties. Groups are everywhere, and we need to learn to work effectively in them to be successful in whatever career path we choose to follow.

PERSPECTIVES ON GROUP DISCUSSION

Experts in a variety of fields study how people behave when working with groups; each discipline approaches the study of groups differently. Some disciplines focus on groups as wholes by de-emphasizing the study of the individual (perhaps by examining how the group affects society). Other disciplines study the individual's experience in a group (perhaps to assess the value of a self-help group). Speech communication takes a prescriptive approach by focusing on the communication behavior associated with effective group processes (to analyze the choices group members make when they communicate in order to improve the outcome).

Our perspective on group discussion focuses on verbal and nonverbal communication choices and assumes that human beings are able to manage both the words that come from their mouths and the behaviors they exhibit. By managing both words and behaviors, people are able to affect the outcomes of situations. We believe that, regardless of the group situation, it is most important for you to manage your own communication responsibly. We will help you make choices regarding your own behavior: what to say, how to say it, to whom, when and where, and with what anticipated effect. We believe you can plan your communication behavior and carry out your plan, and we believe that by learning to do so, you increase your value to the group as well as to yourself. We will also help you make choices about other communication-related behavior: how to listen, lead, manage conflict and participate effectively.

Our purpose in writing this book is to clarify the choices available to improve your effectiveness while participating in discussions. We will suggest things you can do and say to help make group discussion both pleasant and productive. Our advice is directed to members and leaders of numerous discussion groups: educational groups, social groups, and work groups. Our main concern is with you as an individual and with what you can accomplish in a group with other individuals.

WHY DO YOU NEED TO BE AN EFFECTIVE GROUP MEMBER?

In the workplace and in school there are various rewards associated with good group work. If your group is effective, you may gain external rewards such as a monetary bonus, a good grade, or the respect of the supervisor/instructor. If your group is effective, you may gain internal rewards such as pride in your work or increased self-confidence. If you are part of a team, then you may feel that it is your ethical obligation to pull your weight and to be a contributing member of that team. When you perform well in a group situation, you will probably feel good about yourself.

You may also find it valuable to learn to work effectively with groups simply because of the sheer amount of time you will spend in them. Most of us do not like to spend hours and hours performing tasks we are not good at or that we dislike. By learning how to work effectively with groups, you can reduce your stress. Effective group discussion and problem solving is a skill—a skill that most of us do not learn in school. Simply working with groups does not make you an effective group member. You need to learn the tools for being effective and to use these tools in real situations.

HOW TO LEARN ABOUT GROUP DISCUSSION

There are two ways you can learn about discussion. First, you can find a source of information about discussion. This book is such a source. Your class instructor will also be able to provide information. Once you begin to get information, you might begin thinking about what this new information can mean in your life. Examine your past experience with groups. How well did you do in group situations? Did you feel satisfied with your contribution? Were you prepared? Did you have the influence you wanted to have? Did people pay attention to you? Compare your behaviors to those outlined in this book. What do you think you need to learn? Think about the role of discussion in your future career. How will information about group discussion help you when you assume new responsibilities?

The second way to learn is to develop discussion skills through practice. Learning about the skills required of an effective discussion-group member doesn't guarantee that you will be able to perform them. What you need is formal practice and criticism, preferably in a classroom, and a willingness to try your hand at real discussions outside the classroom. By reading and participating and by watching others, you will be able to develop your own style. By listening to criticism from your instructor and others, you will be able to correct your errors and learn more effective ways of behavior.

We do not believe you can learn to master discussion merely by reading about it. We urge you to observe, analyze, and engage in discussion whenever and wherever you can.

WHAT WILL THIS BOOK DO FOR YOU?

This book is the first step in learning the tools that will help you to be effective. The information in the first six chapters applies to all group functions (task, social, educational/self-help groups). We will demonstrate how each member's communication enhances or detracts from the group's experience. To become an effective communicator, you need to understand the choices available and the power of communication.

In the second half of the book, we will elaborate on a particular problem-solving agenda, the standard agenda. By the time you have read chapters 7 through 12 and practiced the steps of the standard agenda, you should be well on your way to improving your performance in task situations.

WHERE WILL YOU USE GROUP DISCUSSION?

Group discussion is prevalent in your life. You can expect to find groups operating no matter where you work or live. Most often, you will participate with groups in education, industry, and community.

In education, groups study for tests, generate research for projects, solve problems in the classroom, and spend late nights griping about instructors and tuition increases. Many campuses offer opportunities to join groups. They may be governing groups like the Student Government Association; social groups like fraternities, sororities, and honor societies; religious groups; or special-interest groups like the geology club or the investment club.

In industry, groups are often assigned tasks dealing with a particular problem, including information about previous attempts to solve it. They may discuss several possible solutions or develop a proposal. They deliver their report to an individual or group responsible for making the final decision. Some companies today are basing their entire organizational structure on teams. A leading data-management company in Arkansas eliminated their hierarchical management structure and created teams. "Once the kinks were worked out of the system, the team structure helped Acxiom significantly shorten decision-making time by allowing the employees closest to each situation to make decisions" (Duffy, 1999, p. 5). In all likelihood, you will experience teamwork in the workforce.

In the community, groups plan fundraising, community service activities, and political action. Candidates use campaign committees to schedule events, develop the tone of the campaign, build the candidate's image, recruit volunteers, and raise money. Lobbying organizations, political activist associations, special interest caucuses, and civic clubs all rely on group discussion to plan activities and to solve problems. Whether you join the Sierra Club, NOW, NAACP, AARP, or the Rotary Club, you will be interacting with others and planning activities to reach a common goal.

FUNCTIONS OF GROUPS

There are many ways to define groups, but we think that it is easiest to categorize groups according to their functions. There are three basic functions of groups.

- *Task* (groups that are formed to gather information, problem solve, or to perform a specific task).
- *Social* (groups that are formed because of a common interest to plan social activities).
- *Educational/self-help* (groups that are formed to help the members learn about something).

Distinguishing a group by its function sounds fairly easy and straightforward; however, many groups serve a variety of purposes. Take a religious student association, for example. This group would be a social group, formed to allow people with the same religious beliefs to gather and to enjoy one another's company. Or is it a learning group because students get together to study and to learn more about scriptures? It might even be a task group if its goal is to recruit new followers.

Internet groups are often defined by more than one function. In a chat room, a social group may get together to discuss a topic of interest. A committee whose members are at different locations could participate online in a chat room, making that group a task group. Let's examine some specific examples of the three functions.

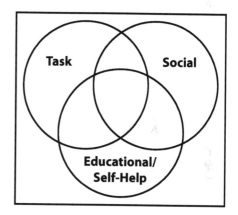

Task Groups

Many groups fall under the heading of task groups because their purpose and function is to govern, solve problems, or complete tasks (examples might include a P.T.A., homeowner's association, or work groups).

Most organization-based task groups are known as *committees*. A committee is a small discussion group that usually has no more than seven or eight members. Committees can be characterized as follows:

- They have a particular task to do as part of a larger organization.
- They meet regularly.
- Members serve on them because of particular knowledge or interest.
- Members are not necessarily linked by personal or social connections.
- The number of members is small enough that they can address each other by name (face-to-face, or via a teleconference call, video-conferencing or computer-mediated discussions).

Industry uses committees for many purposes. Most companies have **standing committees** to deal with matters of finance, membership, and ceremonies and awards, as well as other various ongoing activities. When unforeseen circumstances arrive, *task forces* or *planning groups* are implemented. When there is no plan in place to handle the problem and no group charged with regular responsibility for it, management sets up *ad hoc* committees to define the problem, examine possible effects on the organization, and explore possible solutions. Ad hoc committees may do their job and disband if they are successful, or they may become a standing committee if the problem is ongoing. If committees have more members than can conveniently meet together, they may operate through *subcommittees*. At some point, however, most planning, researching, examining, and proposing is done by a committee.

Local government engages citizens in a variety of committees such as *commissions, authorities, boards, and investigative bodies.* Generally, people serve without pay; it is their way of providing service to the community and having an influence on its future. Such bodies as zoning authorities, planning commissions, school boards, space utilization boards, and other groups that hear citizen complaints, plan for the future, or propose legislation are examples of committees.

> What kinds of committees do you envision yourself serving on in five years?

Social Groups

Social groups generally get together to fulfill human needs to socialize. Few people in our society can function without human interaction on a regular basis. Social groups can range from an informal gathering of friends eating dinner together or talking about instructors to highly-structured social organizations such as fraternities, sororities, religious groups, minority groups, and clubs. Again, their functions overlap. While a fraternity is considered to be a social group, the members also function as a task group if they form a committee to plan a community service project. When they invite a police officer to give a presentation on preventing date rape, they become an educational group.

Educational/Self-help Groups

While a task group focuses on common task goals rather than socializing, and social groups fulfill human needs of communication and belonging, many groups have learning and therapy as goals. These groups differ from task-oriented and social groups because they emphasize personal goals and individual gain. Alcoholics Anonymous, Weight Watchers, and various therapy groups exist so that members can learn about and get help with their problems.

Many self-help groups now operate online in the form of discussion boards. Groups of people with similar interests get together to support one another. As a specific example, Prevention.com has a number of discussion groups. When The South Beach Diet® became popular, a group of people began supporting one another on the Prevention site in 2003. The participants provide tips for eating, but they also share frustrations, eating problems, and many off-topic discussions, including health problems in the family, troubles with children/spouses/parents, etc. The group is available 24-7, and participants never have to leave their homes to stay in touch. It is also easy for participants to get to know one another and gravitate toward people they enjoy. A quick perusal at http://forums.prevention.com/forum.jspa?forumID=40 will show you a number of long-term discussion groups in action.

It is important not to confuse the processes and outcomes of the three types of groups. The goal of educational/self-help groups is to be respectful of individual members' concerns and needs. While that focus could facilitate the interactions of task group members, the primary goal of a task group differs. When setting your own goals, remember to consider the function of your group. In a task group, your best personal gain is the feeling of satisfaction you get from developing a good group solution. In an educational/self-help group, you have the option of setting your own personal goals and using the group to help you achieve them. In a social group, you may want nothing more than some companionship.

What are your task, social, and educational groups this year?

THE VALUE OF PROCEDURE

Sometimes people get together simply to talk—their only goal is to be courteous and friendly. That's fine for social interaction and casual conversation, but it is not useful for task groups in Western culture. Most of corporate America operates on the principle that genuine problem-solving discussion should not be spontaneous and unstructured. For one thing, most people do not have the time to wander aimlessly through a problem. For another, productive discussion requires logical development, mastery of fact, and skill at presentation. An agenda system provides a procedure or method for systematic development of ideas.

An agenda system for group problem solving has a history of success. Douglas Ehninger (1943) stated, "It is generally agreed that the best way to insure the pertinency and adequacy of judgments is to control the thinking process by which they are created" (p. 164). Thomas Scheidel and Laura Crowell (1979) advised, "To be effective for group thinking, communication needs to be characterized by sound thinking and systematic thinking" (p. 52).

Research Check

Scholars continue to suggest that logical, rational, problem-solving groups produce the best solutions. "The results of this study confirm the hypothesis that groups trained in rational problem-solving processes will be judged to have made higher quality decisions than untrained groups. These results support prior research indicating that groups that employ requisite functions outperform groups that do not satisfy such functions" (Schultz, Ketrow, & Urban, 1995, p. 536).

There must be procedure for handling problems. Without a basic structure, discussion becomes rambling and pointless. In such circumstances, it is unlikely that a group will conduct the kind of systematic, thorough investigation necessary for effective decision making. Attention to process is important; process helps determine whether the issues being discussed are the important ones. For this reason, virtually every book on group discussion includes one or more recommended procedures groups can use as a basic plan for their work.

AN INTERCULTURAL NOTE

You may have noticed our reference to American corporate culture. With today's globalization, it is imperative to understand that not everyone subscribes to the view of rational thought.

> Another important consideration in intercultural communication is the influence of culture in cognitive thinking patterns, which includes reasoning and approaches to problem solving. Culture can often produce variant ways of knowing and doing. . . . Northeast Asians (Chinese, Japanese, and Koreans) employ a holistic thinking pattern, whereas Westerners use a linear, cause-and-effect model. To be more explicit, Westerners place considerable value on logical reasoning and rationality. Thus, problems can best be solved by a systematic, in-depth analysis of individual components, progressing individually from the simple to the more complex. Northeast Asians, however, see problems as much more complex and interrelated, requiring a greater understanding of, and emphasis on, the collective rather than focusing on individual parts. (McDaniel, Samovar, & Porter, p. 13).

If group members have different cultural orientations and upbringings, it may be quite difficult for them to solve problems together. The linear problem-solvers will not understand the intuitive method, and those who operate from a collective standpoint will not understand the linear progression. Intercultural understanding is an essential skill in today's global environment.

OVERVIEW OF THE STANDARD AGENDA

Despite increasing globalization, you are probably more likely to encounter problem-solving group discussion in a Western culture, so we will present a formal problem-solving agenda. However, we will try to intersperse some intercultural considerations throughout the discussion. During the early days of group discussion, various authorities attempted to formalize the discussion process around the "five phases of reflective thought" identified by the philosopher John Dewey (1910 and 1933). The steps were originally intended as a description of individual problem solving based on reports by Dewey's students of how they resolved personal problems. Subsequently, speech scholars (i.e. McBurney and Hance; Scheidel and Crowell, as well as many others) turned these descriptive steps into prescriptive models to use during problem-solving group discussions.

In this book we offer you a procedure called the standard agenda. Building on the work of Dewey and others who researched the reflective thinking process, Gerald M. Phillips developed the standard agenda in 1966 to fit management decision-making systems like PERT (program evaluation and review technique) and CPM (critical path method). These systems facilitated the complicated scheduling of manufacturing processes and government administration, and Phillips believed the principles could be translated for all types of groups.

In problem-solving groups, procedures organize discussions and clarify goals. Members will not be willing to give their time and ideas to pursue an abstract goal. In addition, personal goals need to accommodate group goals. For instance, your personal goal might be to leave campus by 2:00 PM each day, whereas your group's goal may be to get an A on the project. Those two goals might end up being incompatible. A leader should have a system in place to direct individual goals and ideas toward common group goals. The first step of the standard agenda focuses you on discussing your personal and group goals plus finding ways to integrate them.

The standard agenda guides both leaders and members in a procedure designed to ensure that their talk relates to matters important to the whole group. It also facilitates systematic study, appropriate word choice, helpful criticism, and constructive conflict. Finally, it provides standards to judge the progress of the group along with guidelines to decide what has been done and what tasks remain to be completed. Above all, the standard agenda makes it possible for a group to work within time limits so it can be responsive to pressure from the company, or legislative body, or institution that needs to have effective solutions to problems delivered on time.

The standard agenda consists of the following steps:

1. *Understanding the charge and each other.* Each group member must understand what the group is to do, why it is important to do it, what the output is to look like, who is to get it, and how the output will be used. The group examines the time frame in which it is to work and schedules itself accordingly. This is also the time to learn about one another so that your group can function as effectively as possible.

2. *Understanding and phrasing the question.* The discussion question guides the problem-solving process. The group must agree on the problem and phrase a question that indicates who is to do what about what. The group must agree on the level or levels of discussion—whether the group is to fact-find, evaluate conditions, set policy, or propose a solution to a problem. A group may do any or all of these.

3. *Fact-finding.* The fact-finding stage allows the group to understand all facets of the problem. The group should gather and record facts after confirming them for accuracy. The group should gather informed opinions from experts. The result should be a statement about the nature of the problem, its relevant history, who is affected and how, what might happen if the problem is not solved, and an estimate of possible causes. At the conclusion of fact-finding, the problem should be summarized and the problem question rephrased, if necessary.

4. *Setting criteria and limitations.* Criteria allow the group to recognize a good solution. The group should list all of the standards which they will use to judge potential solutions. The group should describe what the world would look like if the problem were solved. The group should examine possible limitations that might restrict the solution. The group should anticipate undesirable effects of a solution.

5. *Discovering and selecting solutions.* The group must propose and examine as many solutions as possible and select an optimum solution or construct one from among possibilities after evaluating each against the developed criteria.

6. *Preparing and presenting the final report.* Final reports commonly include: a review of the problem; a review of the problem-solving steps used by the group; a detailed statement of the solution; and an argued defense of the solution.

WHY THE STANDARD AGENDA?

Perhaps you're wondering why we choose to focus on a single discussion procedure. After all, group discussions occur for many reasons. Doesn't it seem reasonable to learn about a variety of procedures? You may think that knowing only one method might limit your effectiveness in different situations. Three reasons contribute to our exclusive focus on the standard agenda. It is the most complete, the most flexible, and a time-tested method for problem-solving discussion.

Complete

An important advantage of the standard agenda is its completeness. The steps in the standard agenda provide a comprehensive understanding of how to solve problems through group discussion. Many newer models presented in group discussion textbooks are actually shortened forms that are less complete. As discussed in the next section, all of the steps may not be necessary for the purpose of a particular group, but the standard agenda offers a complete overview of the problem-solving process when needed.

Flexible

The second advantage of the standard agenda is its flexibility. Leaders and participants can tailor this procedure to fit particular circumstances. Sometimes it's appropriate to omit certain steps. If you're appointed to a fact-finding commission, your goal is restricted to preparing a report on the facts of some situation. You need not develop criteria and limits nor identify and evaluate alternative solutions. Yet, the committee that follows yours might be charged to make recommendations based on your factual report. That committee would omit the opening stages of the standard agenda (covered by your commission) and deal only with the latter phases. Being aware of all components, even if some are omitted, makes it less likely that an important element of the discussion will be overlooked. Learning the most complete and most flexible method permits the group to have the widest range of choices and an informed basis for deciding how thoroughly to apply each step and when to skim or entirely skip parts of the process.

Time-tested

A third and especially persuasive reason for concentrating on the standard agenda is its demonstrated quality over time. Since 1939, when James McBurney and Kenneth Hance introduced a preliminary form of the standard agenda based on Dewey's 1910 writings, the method has been widely used in both training and practice. For at least sixty years the standard agenda has held a prominent position in teaching, research, and consulting.

Business schools, public planning committees, and organizational committees all use the standard agenda. It is also used as a basic form of discussion in the social sciences. It is reasonable to assume that no method could enjoy such wide and sustained popularity unless it led to good results. In a study that compared different problem-solving formats, authors concluded that the model derived from Dewey (the standard agenda) provides an ideal baseline that may be modified to fit particular groups and tasks (Poole, 1981). Whether you are involved in the fact-finding or problem-solving aspect of teamwork (or both), you will find the standard agenda suited to virtually every discussion task you will confront.

THE CHOICES ARE YOURS

Your capacity to manage your communication is one of your most valuable human assets. You have choices to make. Although you may not be able to move mountains, each of you has the ability to influence the people around you—especially when working in groups. Your success with group discussion will be a direct result of the choices you make.

To be an effective communicator, you first need to recognize the opportunities that permit choice and then consider the choices available to you. Among your first choices is the decision to learn more about groups and to become a better participant. No one is born a good discussion-group member. If you learn what is expected of you as a group member and then practice those skills until you are relatively proficient, you expand your capacity to choose a course of action.

You also can make almost unlimited choices about the nature and style of your participation. You need not be locked permanently into one form of behavior or another. In fact, each time you act or don't act, each time you speak or don't speak, each time you offer your comments in a dogmatic tone or with a conciliatory glance or with a high level of enthusiasm, you have made a choice. Consciously or unconsciously, you have decided to do one thing instead of another. Even when your friends expect a particular behavior from you, you have the ability to change. It may take longer to convince people who know you well to accept the fact that you have changed, but you have the ability to make the effort.

You even have a choice about how you use this book. In the next few chapters we will introduce some important concepts about group discussion. We will demonstrate the opportunities for change and give you strategies for effective individual choices in groups. The last six chapters of the book detail the steps of the standard agenda. We will take you step by step through the process, in each case showing you what the group can accomplish and what each member and leader should do to bring about that goal.

If you like, you can move directly to chapter 7 and begin working on discussion problems, saving the next five chapters until later. You may want to alternate chapters, reading chapter 2 and then chapter 8 so you can combine concepts with your practical work using the standard agenda. You might even have a group discussion about the most effective way to use the book. Just keep in mind that learning about discussion does not necessarily make you effective. You must practice these new skills to enhance your participation. Theory and practice go hand-in-hand in learning group discussion. Through it all, the manner in which you communicate is crucial to your development.

Communication choices, of course, may be wise or unwise, effective or ineffective. Each choice you make carries an obligation: the responsibility of accepting the consequences of your actions. If you fail to tell your leader what you want, then you better be prepared for the consequence— accepting whatever is delivered by your leader. Likewise, if you do not take the time to help research your group's problem, then be ready for a superficial and spotty final report that probably will not be accepted. If you use racist, sexist, or heterosexist language, then understand that you may offend others, thus altering the interpersonal dynamics of the group. In each situation you make a choice, and every choice has consequences. It is for this reason that we urge you to consider carefully how you behave and what you say in discussions. You are going to have to live with the consequences your communication style and actions create.

♋ 2 ♋

Understanding the Group as a System

During your lifetime, you've probably taken part in a number of group discussions. Classroom exercises, student organization meetings, griping sessions with friends during lunch, and group assignments all qualify as group discussions. If you're like most people, you've been pleased with your experience in some cases and less satisfied in others. You might find it difficult to explain why some group discussions seemed to be more productive and comfortable than others. It is easy to feel frustrated and confused in group situations and even to conclude that some groups are so chaotic at times that they defy understanding.

Groups are complex. Every group experience is unique because of the variety of influences that operate within it. Understanding groups requires a theoretical perspective that is powerful enough to explain the many simultaneous forces at work. This chapter explains the "systems perspective" of groups and discusses elements that contribute to group effectiveness. Chapter 3 examines factors in the process of group discussion and the outcomes of that discussion. Once you recognize key aspects of group interaction and appreciate the ways they tend to influence individual as well as collective behavior, you'll have a basis for making sound choices regarding your own actions in group situations.

THE SYSTEMS PERSPECTIVE

General systems theory originated with Ludwig von Bertalanffy, a theoretical biologist. The theory analyzes a way to think about and study the constant, dynamic adjustments of living phenomena. His ideas subsequently have been adopted by many social scientists and humanists who seek to understand complicated interpersonal interaction.

According to the theory, an open system (a group, for example) is defined as an organized set of interrelated and interacting parts; the system attempts to maintain its balance amid various influences from the surrounding environment. Think of a flower. A flower is made up of roots, leaves, stem, and buds, all of which are unique, individual parts. However, all of those parts contribute to the nature of the organism. What happens to the roots affects the leaves, stem, and buds. Any outside force in the environment (rain, sun, transplanting, etc.) affects all components of the plant.

Similarly, a group acts as a system made up of many parts (individual members) who all work together to contribute to the experience. No two groups are the same. Even if the same members reconvene in another group experience, the outside forces of the environment (such as breakups, new jobs, different responsibilities, or human development) will affect that group experience. From this model of an open system, we can derive four premises to guide how we think about group discussion.

- Any part of a system can be understood only within the context of the entire system.
- A system is more than the sum of its parts
- All parts of a system interact dynamically and constantly
- An open system interacts with its environment in mutually-influential ways

Any Part of a System Can Be Understood Only within the Context of the Entire System

We cannot isolate one part of a group and try to understand it as its own entity. Discussing only one part of the group context produces distortion. For instance, we cannot account for how a group member acts without considering group norms, the power structure, leadership, and so on. Similarly, to explain a group's decisions we need to analyze member goals, leadership style, resources available to the group, and a host of other factors. For example, Rita may be very quiet in a particular group. Later you see her in another setting in which she is loud and boisterous. How can that be? You thought she was a very shy person. Rita's quietness can only be understood in the context of the specific group in which you observed her. When you look deeper, you find that Rita has no commitment to the first group, and she intensely dislikes the leader who constantly dismisses her ideas. Now Rita's conflicting behavior begins to make sense.

As you participate in discussions, try to avoid analyzing parts of your group out of context. Remember that any component can only be understood in light of the entire system.

Consider this example of a system at your school. The faculty makes decisions regarding teaching methods based on the nature of the students; the nature of the students depends on the tuition; the tuition depends on the funding; the funding affects the morale of the faculty, which in turn affects how they deal with the students, who in turn respond to teaching style, and the cycle repeats.

A System Is More than the Sum of Its Parts

In addition to understanding parts of a system in context, it is also important to note that we cannot understand a group simply by adding up all its separate parts. Simply observing group members, the physical setting, communication patterns, and the decision reached will not give us an accurate picture of what happened. We need to look at the interactions—how physical setting affects members' communication patterns and how the result affects the outcome.

Think of the people in your class. What dynamics are present if you are put in a group with someone with whom you have done many group projects? With someone you don't know? With someone you like? Dislike?

The elements of a group interact dynamically to create new features not present at the outset. For example, Yip may be naturally quiet outside the group, but Lakesha is so friendly and boisterous that the group gets stimulated. Yip and Lakesha develop a relationship unique to a particular group. The group interacts with more than the behavior of Yip plus the behavior of Lakesha; they interact with a Yip/Lakesha dyad. Other members will relate both to the individuals and to their relationship. Over time, the relationships take on new qualities in response to the pattern of communication. For instance, if Yip and Lakesha have a fight, the dynamics in the group will alter. The process reflects the dynamic interactions characteristic of living (open) systems. Once formed, a system engages in an ongoing process of defining and redefining itself, constantly changing as it attempts to sustain itself against internal and external events.

All Parts of a System Interact Dynamically and Constantly

The third premise describes how parts of a group are intricately interconnected; each part affects all others. Many systems theorists point out that a change in any part of a system creates change in all other parts. When one element alters, all others must adjust to accommodate the change if the system is to survive in a healthy state.

> Have you been in a group from which a hardworking, well-liked member suddenly had to resign? How were the dynamics altered in the group?

Some changes have obvious and immediate effects. For example, when Aaron stifles participation in the group, the other members' satisfaction declines. There is a direct relationship between participation and satisfaction. The behavior of a single group member can affect every other member.

> What would be the effect on a group if the boss dropped in to hear a discussion concerning the problems inherent in his or her latest policy proposal?

An Open System Interacts with Its Environment in Mutually Influential Ways

Just as we cannot consider parts of a group in isolation, neither can we consider the group apart from its context. Every group is embedded in many other systems, such as organizations, companies, communities, and cultures. Because they are parts of larger environments, groups both influence their environments and are influenced by them. For example, a committee produces policies for the institution it serves. The institution provides the meeting place and salaries for the committee members. It also shapes member attitudes toward the institution, which are reflected in opinions expressed within the group, which have an impact on the policies the group creates, which affect the institution in ways that affect the members, and so on. Furthermore, members come and go. Each new member brings a new and unique external influence with them. Each departing member changes the shape/tone of the interactions inside the group.

Groups interact with other parts of their environment as well. There is always the potential for conflicts arising from incompatible demands of multiple systems. External obligations may restrict an individual's time and energy to participate effectively, thus producing tension and stress. Individuals sacrifice membership in some of their systems and reduce investment in others, or suffer the consequences of burnout.

People sometimes experience conflicts of interest between the values of two or more systems. It may, for example, be in the interest of an employee's family to keep salaries high; it may be in the interest of the company to keep salaries low. High salaries may put the company out of business, but low salaries may make it difficult for employees to live. How will any given employee respond? Consider the conflicting feelings of a student who cares about and wants to protect the environment, while her parents regularly waste gas and energy. The two systems have clashing values.

Groups must recognize that they operate within an environment. They must stay within the limits of their setting. Too often, groups miss the big picture because they don't recognize the limits of their environment. They decide to change policy without considering the potential problems that change could cause. Groups need to examine the limitations of the organizations, the community, and the culture in which they operate to be effective.

WHY THE SYSTEM MIGHT NOT WORK

There are a variety of reasons why the group might not function effectively as a system. After asking people what problems they have had with groups, we have come up with four of the most frequent complaints.

- Lack of efficiency
- Inhospitable climate
- Inappropriate focus on personal feelings
- Sacrificing personal integrity

Lack of Efficiency

Many people think that some discussions in which they were involved were a waste of time. They believe that groups are not efficient because, rather than working on the task, people "like to hear themselves talk" or because various people "had nothing to say and took too long to say it."

Certainly, discussion can be a waste of time, but not because of some inherent weakness in the process. Nothing magical happens just because people gather together to discuss an issue. Group discussion only works when we make sure that all parts of the system work. For example, our cars are a system—all parts work together. If we don't put gas in our car or change the oil, the car will no longer get us to our destination. That is not because the car is inherently bad; it just needs maintenance. When one group member fails to prepare for a discussion, the group may not have anything useful to say or do. When leaders are not skillful in guiding members in productive directions, discussions will likely degenerate into chaos or pleasant, but nonproductive, bull sessions. When members and leaders do not understand and implement the requirements for effective, purposive discussion, the process will probably be needlessly time consuming and minimally productive.

Inhospitable Climate

There are aggressive talkers everywhere, and most people are not really prepared to compete with them. Many people feel intimidated by conflict and seek to avoid it; others may respond with verbal combat. Usually after being squelched two or three times, a person keeps silent.

However, these difficulties are not inherent in the discussion process. Your members must make careful choices about their own interpersonal behaviors. As you make choices that will affect the climate, you should also keep cultural differences in mind. Some cultures do not speak aggressively or make eye contact. In most Asian cultures, for example, eye contact is a sign of disrespect. If you assume that a person does not want to talk and you ignore him or her, then you will miss out on valuable ideas. Another example that can lead to misunderstanding is that, in general, Caucasian women tend to smile more often than do African-American women (Wood, 2007). While some people may interpret not smiling as inhospitable or excessive smiling as strange, it is important to understand that people have different communication styles. It is important that during the first meeting you talk about how your discussion will proceed and that you are open and ask questions about interpersonal differences.

> What are two things you could tell group members about yourself that would help the group interact better with you and operate more effectively?

Inappropriate Focus on Personal Feelings

A third complaint reflected confusion over the appropriateness and role of personal self-disclosure. While some groups (self-help, for example) focus on the personal feelings of members, doing so in a non-therapeutic context can lead to problems. In a problem-solving group, task aspects should receive primary emphasis. Such an emphasis can also promote friendly and satisfying interpersonal relationships in some cases. By channeling emotions into the hard work of gathering and evaluating information, and by recognizing that a small portion of the meeting should be dedicated to maintenance functions, personal feelings can support problem solving rather than interfere with it. Subsequent chapters will have more to say about the choices regarding the role of personal feelings and the effects of those choices.

Sacrificing Personal Integrity

The fourth complaint, and perhaps the most troublesome of all, came from individuals who felt they had to sacrifice personal integrity in order to work with a group. Often, when five members of the group agree on an idea, the sixth person goes along with the majority to avoid being a holdout. It isn't a consensus at all; the dissenter feels embarrassed by holding out and doesn't want to endure the group's resentment for taking up valuable time.

> Think about a jury. What happens if you disagree with the group? How hard would it be to keep arguing your view? How difficult would it be to give in to the group decision and violate your personal integrity?

It is important for individuals to remain individuals in the group and to feel free to express ideas. Group process is designed to synthesize individual ideas to obtain "the greatest good for the greatest number." Individual points of view cannot be synthesized unless they are expressed. Notice how a productive climate ties directly to this complaint as well. If individuals do not feel encouraged to express dissenting views, then they will not, and it is the group who will lose.

MAKING THE SYSTEM WORK

Good group discussion does not just happen automatically; group members must work at it. Our view is rhetorical; we believe that individuals can make things happen by saying what needs to be said when it needs saying. It also means that we make some assumptions about what happens in discussion. We will cover five basic premises of effective group discussion.

- Effective discussion is goal oriented
- Effective discussion is regulated by a public agenda
- Effective discussion requires that every member be responsible for the group's effectiveness
- Effective discussion presumes cooperative efforts and attitudes
- Effective discussion requires leadership

Effective Discussion Is Goal Oriented

When we talk about group discussion, we do not include all the things people can do together in groups. We are not concerned with casual socialization or group therapy. For our purposes, a small number of people gathering and sharing ideas does not make group discussion, even though it may qualify as a group conversation.

When we talk of group discussion, we are dealing with a relatively formal process. It is specific talk by people who have formed groups to make decisions, to solve problems, to declare policy, to evaluate programs, to collect and examine facts, to administer operations, to select personnel, and so forth. The kind of group problem solving that we detail in this book almost always requires some kind of formal outcome.

It doesn't matter whether your group is in the corporate sector, the community, or the classroom or whether members have volunteered or have been assigned. The kind of discussion we are writing about is purposive activity intended to accomplish some goal that the individual acting alone could not attain or that no single individual could handle because so many people have an interest in the outcome.

> **Research Check**
>
> "We found that goal setting is positively related to team performance, as measured by efficiency and effectiveness" (Hoegl & Parboteeah, 2003).

Effective Discussion Is Regulated by a Public Agenda

Group discussion requires that a number of people with different ideas and points of view come together and talk in order to solve problems. Due to the volume of different ideas, it is important to have procedures that all participants can follow. These "rules of order" will help members focus on the task in a systematic, effective way. Procedural rules help reduce conflict and uncertainty and help members focus on a common goal. When discussion participants follow an agenda, they can process their ideas intelligently and increase their chances of achieving a workable solution to the problem (see box on p. 23).

Effective Discussion Requires That Every Member Be Responsible for the Group's Effectiveness

Earlier in this chapter, we talked about the premise that a system is more than the sum of its parts. This is true only if all of the parts are working properly (as in our car example). All too often groups are composed of some individuals who abdicate personal responsibility. They arrive unprepared and don't participate. Yet, at the end of the project, they feel free to criticize everyone else.

To be effective, members must be committed to listen, to think through, to reason, and to share the results of their reasoning with the group. All members must adopt a critical attitude toward the information

The typical order of business is as follows (Sturgis, 2001, p. 114):

1. Call to order
2. Reading, correction, approval, or disposition of minutes of previous meeting
3. Reports of officers
4. Reports of boards and standing committees
5. Reports of special committees
6. Unfinished business
7. New business
8. Announcements
9. Adjournment

If you are working on an informal task force or committee, you won't need steps 3–5. Be sure to understand that individual items should be listed in numbers 6, 7, and 8. You may also want to have a time limit allotted to each item if long meetings are a problem.

they collect and that which is presented by others. To do this, all members must know what is expected, what possibilities exist for behaviors and, most important, how to separate the personal from task issues. Members should realize that when someone is critical of their ideas, the spirited discussion will help the group make a better decision. It is not a personal attack. When each member takes responsibility to listen carefully and to question the information and ideas, critical communication will be a welcome norm, and groups should end up with better ideas and solutions.

Effective Discussion Presumes Cooperative Efforts and Attitudes

Group discussions are not forums in which individuals may orate on behalf of their favorite causes or charities. They require participation around a common agenda. As a member of a discussion group, you are obligated to have ideas about the topic or question under discussion. You are obligated to present those ideas and to listen to the ideas of others. You are entitled, even urged, to criticize ideas, dissent when it is reasonable, and argue when you are legitimately motivated to do so. Keep in mind, though, that your goal is not to "defeat" or "critique" the people who disagree with you, but for each of you to come closer to a common position. This will help your group to achieve the cooperative spirit of group discussion.

Effective Discussion Requires Leadership

Someone needs to be responsible for making the process work. In problem-solving groups, someone must be responsible for the following.

- Oversee liaisons with agencies.
- Coordinate work that is assigned.
- Make sure work gets completed.
- Keep records.
- Keep participation going in the group.
- Referee conflicts.
- Maintain files of information and ideas.
- Notify the group of time and place of meetings.

Above all, someone must lead. While discussion groups can distribute leadership tasks among members, we advocate having a central person responsible for overseeing these tasks. There are many ways to select a leader and many responsibilities for the leader to perform. We will focus on them in depth in another chapter.

In this chapter, we have reviewed the systems perspective, what happens when the system doesn't work, and how to make the system work. Next we will identify three integral parts of the system.

✂ 3 ✂

Exploring the Group System

We've summarized the systems approach to small-group problem solving and the possible reasons why the system either works or does not work. In order to further understand the systems approach, we'll examine the three components of group systems: (1) the initial elements, (2) the process elements, and (3) the outcomes.

Small-Group System and Surrounding Environment		
Initial Elements	*Process Elements*	*Outcome Elements*
• Group size	• Participation	• Effectiveness of group decisions
• Group charge	• Group roles	• Individual satisfaction
• Resources	• Norms	• Changes in environment
• Individual members	• Power	
	• Cohesion	
	• Decision-making style	
	• Group autonomy	

Initial Elements

Any group system is composed of four initial elements: the group size, the group charge, the group's resources, and the characteristics of individual members.

Group Size

The size of a group influences the process and outcomes of problem solving. Based on the early work of Robert Bales (1954), most authorities believe that a group with five to seven members is the ideal size. With less than five, a group lacks diverse opinions, thus losing a broad perspective and consideration of various ideas. In groups of four or less, members may fear that they will alienate their colleagues, so they may be reluctant to disagree; that sense of closeness occasionally impedes critical, reflective analysis of issues. Groups with more than seven members should watch for signs of factions and subgroups forming that might disrupt the group. When groups divide naturally, power plays, domination, and dissatisfied members often result. Therefore, you may want to think about dividing into sub-committees to ease the tension and confusion of a large group trying to meet during the early stages of research and discussion. As an alternative, you could implement some formal rules for participation so that everyone is heard.

Group Charge

A charge is the official task given to the group. It is not possible for a group to be effective unless all members understand the task and the expected final outcome. Unfortunately, organizations and the people responsible for assigning group tasks are not always clear in explaining why the group was formed and what is wanted as the final output. Understanding the group's purpose is crucial to success. An added benefit to a clearly stated charge is that the common group goal should unify members. Groups need to ask the person in charge for clarification if there is any disagreement among group members when interpreting the charge. A group tends to falter when its members lack a clear purpose or when they disagree about their purpose. Members may become disillusioned when the group becomes paralyzed due to confusion. Strange as it sounds, some groups have worked for weeks or months on a charge, only to find out that they misinterpreted the task or outcome.

Resources

Resources are another element the group should consider at the outset. What resources are available? Resources come in many forms. Is there a meeting space and office supplies? What, if any, is the budget? What skills will each member contribute? How can the group secure help with skills they do not possess? Do they have access to emotional support if it is necessary? Does the person giving the charge support them? These are just a few of the resource areas a group can analyze before beginning their task.

Individual Members

Groups are made up of individuals who have unique personalities, needs, abilities, and self-esteem. These attributes impact the participation style of each member, which in turn influences the group.

PERSONALITIES AND NEEDS

Lupita has a high need for order and achievement but cares little about getting recognition for a job well done. Heather, on the other hand, needs to have someone compliment her on each and every step of a task. She has a lot of affiliation needs (such as wanting to be in the group to socialize with the other members). Because those needs are so strong, she sometimes guides the group away from the task. How do you think these two members will get along with each other?

> List your needs as a group member. Think about your goals for participating. Are they similar to the needs and goals of other members? Dissimilar? Would you prefer to work with Heather or Lupita?

Although there is no profile of a perfect group member, effective group work depends on the ability of each member to tolerate one another. How do you find out about individual members? One important strategy is to discuss personal characteristics and needs at the initial meeting. Who is self-motivated? Who needs external motivation? Who needs compliments? Who does not? Who is a dominant communicator? Who is a passive communicator? If Michael knows that two of his group members need a lot of positive reinforcement, he can then make the choice to provide it or to think carefully about why he decides not to do so. But he can't make an effective choice if he does not know the information or if he assumes that all members operate in the same way that he does. The success of this strategy will depend on the willingness of members to provide accurate information about themselves.

> How comfortable do you feel with identifying and sharing your needs with others? Why?

ABILITIES

A second strategy to discover information about individuals is to inventory the skills and abilities of group members in order to determine their areas of competency. Some groups make the mistake of having everyone work equally on all aspects of the problem. However, if one person excels at library research while another prefers interviewing people, then it makes sense to assign individual tasks accordingly. Be sure that your group takes advantage of each member's skills.

> Brainstorm a list of skills that would be necessary for a group to have in order to complete the task that you have been assigned. (If you have no assignment, your instructor can give you a sample task).

SELF-ESTEEM

Sometimes members want to know why other members act the way they do. There is no easy answer to this question. Self-concept is what you think of yourself—your physical characteristics, skills, abilities, and personal qualities. Self-esteem is the way you feel about those things based on the value you give to those qualities. Self-concept and self-esteem have a tremendous impact on member participation. If Claire doesn't see herself as a contributor (self-concept) or if she doesn't think she has valuable things to say (self-esteem), then she won't participate in the group.

Those who have high self-esteem are willing to take risks in offering ideas, can take criticism, assume their share of blame, and take credit graciously. By contrast, people with low self-esteem tend to be hypercritical of themselves and others, defensive about their worth and efforts, pessimistic about what the group can achieve, and in constant need of assurance of their merit.

DIVERSITY

Diversity can make a difference in an individual's performance as well. If you have someone in your group from an Asian culture, chances are they will be less likely to jump into spirited discussion because of their cultural norms. If you have someone from a collectivistic culture,

> Luis Amaral, a physicist at Northwestern University, researched the human dynamics of teamwork with sociologist Brian Uzzi and other colleagues. "We looked at what made teams successful in several areas. We found that teams that were successful brought together some new people as well as experienced people who never worked together before. So it was a diversity of perspectives that made a team successful and pairing a variety of people that kept ideas fresh. The unsuccessful teams, on the other hand, paired the same people together over and over" (Jones, 2006).

they will approach group work in a far different way than someone from an individualistic culture. If you have someone from an Eastern culture, they may be less likely to work well with the reflective-thinking process described in this book—instead they may rely on a more intuitive problem-solving model because of a difference in global thinking patterns.

People's time orientations affect their group performance as well. Edward Hall (1966) described two contrasting ways to treat time. Monochronic cultures structure time into discrete units (minutes and hours) and treat it like an object. People compartmentalize time, structure formal appointments, feel pressured by time, and operate on a tight schedule. In polychronic cultures, time is unstructured and informal. The rhythms of nature mark the flow of time. Tasks are completed no matter how long they take, and people may be hours late for their next meeting. This causes no stress, and people wait patiently. If you work with someone from a polychronic culture, they'll be less concerned with time limits and meeting starting times than people who are from monochronic cultures. Being aware of the backgrounds of the individuals you are working with can make group discussion go much more smoothly.

PROCESS ELEMENTS

Group members, size, and purpose interact dynamically to create new elements that further affect the process and outcomes of problem-solving discussion. We will discuss seven process elements of interaction: participation, group roles, norms, power, cohesion, decision-making style and group autonomy.

Participation

Participation is probably the single most important influence on a group's ability to operate and achieve. Because members are brought together to discuss a problem, it is most desirable for a group to have relatively equal participation by all members. Participation is important for three reasons. First, there is a greater chance that important ideas will be expressed. Second, because participation is closely related to satisfaction, there is a greater chance that members will be pleased with their participation. Third, members are likely to become committed to the group and its outcomes. People are more willing to implement solutions they helped shape.

You cannot, however, estimate the *quality* of talk by the *amount* of talking. The person who talks most is not necessarily the person who contributes the most. Although productive group members talk often, conversational bullies and time wasters may also dominate the group. In evaluating effectiveness, your group must evaluate both quantity and quality of participation; your group must also recognize a member's listening effectiveness as an integral part of communication.

How would you do the following in a group?
- Quiet a talkative member.
- Encourage a quiet member.
- Handle a group where everyone speaks at the same time.
- Handle a group where no one speaks.

There are intercultural differences that influence one's participation as well. If your personal physical characteristics make you a minority in the group, you may be less likely to feel comfortable participating. If you come from a culture that values respect toward elders or people of status (i.e., a leader) you may be unlikely to point out flaws in others' ideas or play devil's advocate (someone who takes an unpopular position to provoke discussion, regardless of whether they support the position or not).

Each member is personally responsible for creating balance in the group. It is important to make it possible for quiet members to participate, to discourage those who speak a lot, and to avoid dominating the conversations. It is also important to recognize that listening is just as important as talking.

Group Roles

When people participate in a group, they perform various roles: task, procedural, and climate. Each role impacts the group as a system.

- *Task roles* involve communicating the information necessary to solve the problem: asking for ideas and information, giving ideas and information, and elaborating and evaluating information that has been introduced into deliberations. Each of these task roles assists a group in its effort to gain valid, reliable information on which to base a sound decision.

- *Procedural roles* organize the group: establishing and maintaining the agenda, coordinating various ideas, summarizing progress, and recording key ideas and agreements. Procedural roles are marked by comments that help members stay on course.

- *Climate roles* contribute to creating and maintaining a healthy, cooperative tone. They include recognizing others' ideas, reconciling conflicts, releasing tension in the group through humor or other means, and emphasizing collective goals and values. A climate role can help sustain an atmosphere conducive to cooperative, productive discussion.

Think about which roles you enjoy and in which you excel. Task-oriented people like to research, analyze, evaluate, and synthesize. They put together reports, design presentations, and create output. If you enjoy the task roles you may want to consider being the researcher or holding another important job in the group. If you also enjoy procedural roles, you may want to be the leader.

If you like to organize and keep track of the work progress, then you might enjoy a procedural role. Notice that someone who enjoys organizing may also choose to be the leader. Recorders fill a vital procedural role when they take minutes for the meeting and keep track of the ideas, the discussion, and the decisions. People who excel at procedural roles enjoy creating agendas and making sure members stick to them. They often remind the group members to stay focused if any drift off track.

People who excel at climate roles have excellent interpersonal skills. They may be quite social and enjoy the relationships that are forming in the group. They may have a knack for noticing when there is tension in the group and relieve it with an appropriate, well-timed joke, compliment, or observation. They are well versed in conflict-resolution strategies (discussed in chapter 6) and can use them effectively.

> As a group, discuss which roles you are most comfortable with and why. A healthy group has a good mix of people who can perform various roles.

The fourth communication role is unproductive and undesirable. *Egocentric roles* reflect individual concerns and interests and often hinder collective communication. Examples of egocentric roles are personal socialization, refusing to permit the group to move on, seeking personal attention and recognition, making personal attacks on others, pleading for special interests, bringing up personal concerns, and withdrawing from participation. Any behavior that places personal concerns above those of the group should be discouraged.

> What are some of the real-world examples of egocentric roles that you have encountered?

Norms

Groups form habits just as individuals do. Once people have been together for a time, they develop norms—standardized ways of managing tasks, procedures, and climate. Norms are patterns of beliefs, attitudes, communication, and behavior within groups. They grow out of member interaction and then, in systematic fashion, influence group interaction.

Norms are important because, once they are established, members know what is acceptable and unacceptable behavior in the group. Keep in mind, however, that some established norms can be extremely counterproductive. For instance, a norm may develop where some group members publicly humiliate other members or where half of the group continuously comes to meetings late. Obviously, these norms would be counterproductive. It is important to confront and resolve potential pitfalls and/or to make rules about problems as soon as they arise.

For effective group interaction, members must adhere to norms. They provide guidelines for members to disagree in acceptable ways, resolve conflicts, release tension, welcome new members, and do business. Let's say that a norm for your discussion group is to arrive on time. What happens when Miguel arrives 10 minutes late for one meeting? Members may voice concern; they assume that something kept him from complying with the norm. What happens when he arrives late for the fourth time in a row?

Norms form at the beginning of group interaction and are easiest to modify at the outset. Once norms have operated long enough they become a part of a group's identity and are difficult to change. Effective groups pay attention to the norms from the beginning.

Let's look at some common norms. Some groups socialize for five to ten minutes; some begin by reading minutes from the previous meeting; others expect the leader to begin by reviewing the agenda. In some groups interaction is very formal, while in others it is casual and free-flowing. In some groups members are very attentive to the person speaking, while in other cases interruptions are frequent and accepted. You should be able to make a connection between norm formation and developing a productive communication climate. When possible, you should modify any norms that seem inappropriate or counterproductive to your group.

If members do not conform to norms, conflict may start to escalate and group members may become dissatisfied. For instance, if the norm is to come to the meeting prepared but Rachel consistently violates this norm, the other members may begin to resent her. Members who do not conform to norms are usually punished informally. Most groups, however, first try to alert the nonconforming member that his/her behavior is inappropriate. In Rachel's case, the leader might make a little joke, "So nice you could join us," or may pull her aside to let her know her behavior is unacceptable. Next the group may punish the person by refusing to listen to his/her ideas. Finally, the group may withdraw the privilege of membership, either formally by expelling the member or informally by failing to send notifications of meeting time and place.

For participation to be effective, it is important that you recognize group norms. Once identified, you can make informed choices about when to conform, when not to, and when to comment on norms. Keep in mind that norms should be examined periodically. Often a new member might have a fresh perspective and ask why the group has a certain norm.

This is the perfect opportunity to examine and discuss taken-for-granted behaviors. The response "because it's always been done that way!" is not particularly helpful. Because all group members are expected to conform to most norms most of the time, you should weigh the value of membership carefully and evaluate the norms. If you do not have the option to leave the group (i.e., in a class assignment), then you may want to try to alter the norms.

Research Check

How do you go about establishing norms in online groups? Charles Graham (2003) examined online teams. "The study described a norming process that typically began with teams establishing general norms with fuzzy boundaries and then modifying the norms over time to make them more operationalized by more specifically articulating the norm boundaries [communicate frequently becomes check email every morning and evening]. . . . It is possible that understanding how the norming process works, along with some idea of critical norm content for computer-mediated teamwork, could help facilitate the rapid development of key norms in an on-line environment. One of the implications of this is that teams would be able to spend more time engaged in work or learning activities and less time in conflict resolutions and other group dynamics activities" (p. 351).

Power

We define power as the ability to influence others. Sometimes occupying a position makes a person powerful (leader in the group, for example). A person may also earn power by demonstrating competence or expertise in a particular area or subject. At other times people have power because of their status in a company or in society. It is important to recognize who has power in the group so that you can make sure it is not abused.

In an ideal situation power is distributed equitably among group members; however, there may be one or more people in a group who have substantial power. For instance, let's say that you are on a company committee with your supervisor. The supervisor may be perceived as having more power in that group because other members may be reluctant to challenge his/her ideas. Members with power can influence decisions. Leaders also have power by virtue of their position. While it would make sense to trust an expert member's judgment, you want to be careful about accepting ideas just because the person who proposed them is powerful. If members succumb automatically to people who have power, the group process can be greatly disrupted. It is up to the members to carefully guard against any inappropriate influence.

You should also be aware that a reciprocal relationship exists between participation and power. Often, members who posses power participate more than those with little power. This inequity can make the less influential people feel inadequate and eventually cause them to become hostile or to leave. This hurts the group because it eliminates a potential contributor.

Another type of group member uses his or her communication to achieve power. Sometimes people who rarely speak are looked upon as having great knowledge. This may or may not be accurate. Other people may use a boisterous communication style to gain power. Their dynamic communication style distracts the group from analyzing the content of their talk.

Cohesion

Cohesion refers to the "feeling of we-ness" in a group—a team orientation. In cohesive groups, members generally pull together and agree on major issues such as the nature of the task and the goals they hope to achieve. The characteristics of a moderately cohesive group are that its members work hard, are satisfied with what they do, find the group comfortable, and respect one another. In groups lacking cohesiveness, members tend to be less willing to invest effort toward any group goals; there is less satisfaction with the group; respect may be minimal; and there may be a chilly, even antagonistic and competitive climate.

At times, a group can experience too much or too little cohesion. Too much cohesion tends to subvert individuality and often deprives the group of independent, critical, and creative thought. We have seen student groups who were so cohesive and felt so connected to one another that they rarely completed any work. Too little cohesion may result in a group that has no common objectives, beliefs, and motivations. Effective problem solving requires a healthy balance between cohesion and individuality.

Keep in mind that cohesion is not necessarily characteristic of an entire group. Sometimes only part of a group is cohesive, or there may be

Research Check

In a study that questioned 105 athletes, "It was found that approximately 56% of the respondents indicated that there could be disadvantages to high social cohesion. On the other hand, approximately 31% of the respondents indicated that there could be disadvantages to high task cohesion" (Hardy, Eys, & Carron, 2005, p. 172). Some of the perceived disadvantages of social cohesion in sports teams included time wasting and decreased focus. For high task cohesion, some of the disadvantages included reduced social relations, incompatible attitudes, and perceived pressures.

two cohesive factions within a single group. Usually this happens when groups become too large to allow the informal, interactive communication conducive to building a sense of team. As the inner group becomes increasingly cohesive, it also becomes a clique that prevents others from contributing to the progress of the overall unit.

So how can your group develop cohesion? We will discuss three guidelines for developing cohesion.

- Encouraging a sense of belonging to the group.
- Reminding the group of shared needs, interests, and goals.
- Using interpersonal rewards.

When members truly value belonging to a group, the group will generally be more cohesive. People usually feel more "connected" to some groups than to others. If group members are assigned to a task that they do not care a lot about, the group may need to encourage a feeling of belonging. One way to do this is to develop a group name, common theme, or slogan. Your group can do this in one of the initial meetings to break the ice and to get to know one another. Sometimes the simple act of developing a name, themes, and slogans helps to bond the group. Use of these items throughout the project helps the group to remain cohesive.

To develop a name, theme, or slogan, think about the purpose of the group, commonalities among members, or accomplishments that the group hopes to achieve. We had one group who labeled themselves the "A-Team" because they remembered the television show with that title, and they wanted to achieve an "A" on their project. Another group at the University of Central Arkansas wanted to keep the UCA letters, so they named themselves "Undergraduate Communication Association." Their slogan was "In pursuit of a degree of solutions." We have had groups who talked about getting T-shirts, etc. with their name or slogan on them. This kind of talk and activity helps to build cohesion, and it isn't just for students. Building cohesion through development of a name, theme, or slogan either formally or informally is used in the business world as well.

Another way to build cohesion is to talk about and remind each other of shared needs, interests, and goals. The idea is to get agreement on the goals and methods of procedure, and to encourage disagreement on facts and solutions. If the group shares a goal (i.e. to get an "A," to build a new community park for children, etc.) then the cohesion tends to be higher in the group. When the going gets tough or the workload seems to be impossible, being reminded that "we are doing this for the kids" or "remember we all want to succeed on this project" can be motivators that continue the cohesion of the group. Most members don't change their minds about goals midstream. You generally would not hear someone say "I don't care about the kids anymore." So reminding each other of the shared goals can help the group's cohesiveness. In addition, encouraging members to disagree openly without criticism can do a lot to help people feel comfortable in the group.

The third way to build cohesion is through interpersonal rewards. Many people seek a group that confirms them personally by providing acceptance and a sense of belonging. Individuals may be willing to work hard and effectively on a task in exchange for the privilege of being accepted in a group. Most people, in fact, seek some personal confirmation. In really effective groups, members encourage each other by taking note of exceptional contributions. Simple acknowledgements such as "good idea," "I like that," "great, I wouldn't have thought of that," or "yes, that makes much more sense" help members to feel good about their contributions. Written affirmations are also helpful. A simple e-mail to members thanking them for their contributions can go a long way toward building and maintaining cohesion in the group. Recently a member of a local PTA received a hand-written thank you note for helping out at an event when another member canceled at the last moment. The member who wrote the note did a lot for the cohesion of the group. The recipient felt great and was willing to help out again. The recipient's wife was pleased and felt good about the group leading to a public commendation of the note writer at the next meeting, which in turn promoted more good will. Try to think about what kinds of interpersonal rewards would work in your group.

Research Check

Karin Sanders and Aukje Naute (2004) found that gender may make a difference in cohesion. "Significant correlations were found regarding the degree of similarity with respect to gender and the frequency of informal meetings, closeness of the informal relationships, and cohesiveness within a team. This means that we can confirm Hypothesis 1: similarity with respect to gender is positively related to cohesiveness within the team" (p. 732).

Sanders and Naute also confirmed their third hypothesis that "the more cohesive a team, the lower the short-term absenteeism of the employees within the team" (p. 734). This study was done on a real-world work group. These findings demonstrate the importance of cohesiveness in a work environment—both in school groups and the work world.

One word of caution, however, if the group gets too "congratulatory" and loses its ability to think sharply and be critical of ideas, then this overly-cohesive group may find itself with a less than satisfactory solution. Chapter 6 discusses three ways to create a constructive climate that will help your group enhance its cohesion.

Decision-Making Style

Decision-making style usually develops as a norm. We will cover three methods of reaching decisions in groups, each of which may be appropriate in particular circumstances.

Consensus is the unanimous agreement of all members. It preserves group unity and member commitment if it was reached through consideration of complex issues. The major drawback of seeking consensus is that it can be time consuming. For important policy issues central to the group's work, time spent seeking consensus may be a sound investment. On minor issues, consensus may consume more time than appropriate, and when there are emergencies the group may have to act so quickly that seeking consensus is not possible. A second potential weakness of consensus is that it can result in uninspired decisions because they have been so watered down by the compromises necessary to secure unanimous agreement.

A second method, *negotiation*, involves bargaining among members to build a solution that honors each person's position on particular issues. One member may be willing to bend on cost in exchange for others agreeing to a particular plan for implementing recommendations. Negotiating a solution usually takes less time than consensus, and it can result in bolder decisions, since not all members have to agree with all aspects of the solution. Its primary advantage is that it accommodates parties with divergent and even conflicting goals and allows them to come up with a reasonable agreement that everyone can accept.

For example, one of the authors recently allowed an upper-division class to decide on a due date for a group paper. Half the class wanted it to be due on Friday so that they wouldn't have to think about it over the weekend, while the others wanted it due on Monday so that they would have more time to work. Neither side would budge, and consensus was impossible. However, they negotiated an agreement in which we decided to put an extra member in one group. This group would have a Friday deadline. The other groups would be slightly smaller and would have the Monday deadline. While this wasn't what the instructor had in mind, everyone was happy with the solution. Negotiation, however, can have several drawbacks, including its tendency to result in piecemeal solutions that are sometimes less coherent than consensual decisions.

A third method is formal or informal *voting*. The obvious advantage of voting is efficiency; it is a quick, decisive means of settling issues. Be cautious that high-powered individuals do not pressure others into voting their way. This is a time when you want to be aware of certain members' power within the group. Another disadvantage is that voting may create divisions in a group, polarizing winners and losers and generating resentment, frustration, and disillusionment.

None of these methods is best. Each has its strengths and limitations, and each can be useful in particular circumstances. What is important is that members understand that there are alternative styles of making decisions and that they appreciate the probable impacts of each style. Make informed choices as you use the various styles.

Group Autonomy

Over the course of problem solving, members come to see their group in particular ways. Just as individuals develop self-images, groups develop some sense of identity or image. Central to identity is the degree to which members perceive their group as autonomous. Autonomy refers to the degree to which a group can operate independent of external controls, constraints, and directives for outcomes. If group members believe their group has little real power and exists merely to ratify what some superior has already decided, then motivation drops, creativity diminishes, and the quality of solutions is impaired. By contrast, when members think they do have power and responsibility as relatively independent agents, the result is likely to be a motivated, enthusiastic, and effective group.

> Have you been in a group where you had to make a decision, but you knew that no one would consider it seriously? How did that affect your performance in the group?

Most groups have some autonomy. Total autonomy or a total lack of autonomy is rare. The perception of a fair degree of independence is critical to committed, effective problem solving. Members may create a sense of autonomy or an image of the group as a rubber stamp through their communicative choices. The tone and content of communication during discussion reveals attitudes toward autonomy. Members who constantly refer to outside attitudes or to the effect of the group on its organization, or who seem to look over their shoulders for approval from reference groups, do not have an autonomous image.

As the group characteristics—individuals, size, and purpose—interact dynamically, new features evolve. We have discussed the seven process elements: participation, group roles, norms, power distribution, cohesion, decision-making style, and group autonomy. Remember that each of these system process elements interacts with all others in complex and dynamic ways. In addition, all the features we have examined so far influence the outcomes of problem-solving deliberations, which is the focus of the final section of this chapter.

OUTCOME FEATURES

What are the outcomes of group problem-solving discussion? What results from the interactions we have described thus far? Three end results of discussion merit our attention: effectiveness of group decision, individual satisfaction, and change in the environment surrounding a group. All of these outcomes are interrelated, each affecting all others.

Effectiveness of Group Decisions

The first discussion outcome is group decision. The effectiveness of a group's final product is, after all, the bottom line in evaluating the group's success. Many groups think that they should be rewarded for their effort. One of the authors tells students, "T + E ≠ A." In other words, time plus effort does not necessarily equal an "A" on an assignment. Groups can spend a lot of time developing a less than satisfactory solution. Often the person who assigned the task is much more concerned with the solution than with how much time and effort a group put into developing it. What matters is whether it can be implemented effectively and whether there will be collateral effects, creating other problems.

Effective decisions tend to be based on sound information and reasoning, and they tend to have a substantial base of support from members and from people outside the group who will affect implementation. Usually it takes a great deal of time before a solution devised by a group can be thoroughly tested. During that time new problems may arise, and the solution is modified to respond to changing conditions.

Individual Satisfaction

Member satisfaction is the second discussion outcome. It is an important measure of a group's effectiveness. How positively members feel about their group may be affected by a variety of factors, most of which we have already examined. Topping the list of influences on satisfaction is participation. Satisfaction tends to be positively related to the amount of talk in which a member engages. Further, power is associated with participation, so it is indirectly related to satisfaction. Cohesion is another influence on satisfaction, since members tend to take pleasure in belonging to a tightly knit team. Similarly, participatory decision-making methods generally enhance satisfaction, while more autocratic or divisive methods hamper individuals' contentment with the group process.

Other factors that promote satisfaction are recognition, responsibility, interest in the task, and group achievement. If a group is successful and members feel they actively contributed to that success, satisfaction is likely to be high. Individual satisfaction is very complex. Success of the group motivates commitment to it. Commitment makes a member work harder. Hard work, in turn, improves the solution. There is so much involved in the issue of member satisfaction that it is central to the issue of group effectiveness.

> **Research Check**
>
> Surprise!
> "Interestingly, the results [of this study] indicated that the formation of trust is not necessary for a virtual team to deliver a quality result. Some teams showing low levels of trust were able to provide high quality output. It seems that one explanation of this lack of relationship between trust and performance may reside in the notion of process loss or gain. Although some low trust teams might have delivered high-quality results, they may have expended significantly more effort to do so than did high trust teams" (Aubert & Kelsey, 2003, p. 605).

Changes in Environment

Finally, problem-solving discussion normally occurs in an open system in which there is exchange between a group and its environment. There are two significant ways that groups influence their contexts.

First, a group that engages in careful, informed problem solving is likely to generate solutions that alter the environment by eliminating or reducing the problem that originally brought members together. For example, student groups in discussion classes at one university successfully enlarged the orientation for transfer students, modified the procedure that financial aid students must follow to buy textbooks, participated in revising the public relations program for the campus counseling center, and even developed a proposal for enhancing the edition of the book you are reading. Any serious problem-solving effort can alter policies and make an impact on the environment.

A second way in which problem solving affects the surrounding environment is through the group's impact on individual members. Through participation members become informed on issues; they learn of alternative solutions and the promises and pitfalls of each. As a result of intense deliberation, members often become advocates of particular solutions and the values embedded in them. Thus, they are changed personally by their involvement in discussion. In addition, members may act as agents of change to influence the attitudes of others with whom they interact. During and after problem solving, members deal with people outside the group, and they influence what those people will know, believe, and endorse. This happens not only through formal advocacy of the group's recommendations, but also through informal conversations with colleagues, friends, and family. Grassroots organizations consider this sort of interpersonal persuasion between people to be a primary source of changes in broad social values. Thus, the environment surrounding a group is affected by actual decisions reached and by the presence in that environment of informed individuals who influence the attitudes, opinions, and actions of others.

In this chapter we have reviewed the initial elements, the process elements, and the outcome elements of a small group as a system. Next we will examine individual choices that enhance or detract from these elements.

✍ **4** ✍

Individual Choices That Affect the System

Choices are the foundation on which this entire book is based. Choices are also the foundation for an effective communicator. People make choices based on insight and knowledge about a particular situation and the other people involved. This chapter will cover a number of areas in which you can make effective choices that will affect the group.

RHETORICAL SENSITIVITY

A rhetorically-sensitive group member considers the needs of the receiver and sends a message in a manner that does not offend. Roderick Hart and Don Burks (1972) originally introduced this concept, and we use their excellent foundation in applying their ideas to discussions.

When you are rhetorically sensitive, you encourage others to cooperate. The following five principles communicate rhetorical sensitivity:

1. **I am aware of your existence and declare your importance and uniqueness.** Members communicate this attitude by listening carefully, remaining calm and patient, allowing others to talk, and asking intelligent questions. You demonstrate courtesy by maintaining eye contact when listening and by keeping an open mind and a positive attitude. You can choose to foster an atmosphere of respect for one another. Keep in mind that it is possible to respect people with whom you disagree. ("Wow, I really disagree with that idea because of . . ." vs. "You are wrong!")

2. **I believe in what I am saying.** By speaking vigorously and preparing in advance, you communicate that you believe what you are saying. There is no point in talking if you don't have something

43

substantial to say. If you talk without having a contribution to make, you are taking time away from other members; so think carefully, speak thoughtfully, and be willing to share your information and views when appropriate.

3. **We are all going to get something out of this.** A rhetorically sensitive communicator does not present ideas in a "win-lose" style. You can demonstrate an attitude of camaraderie by explaining your point of view, showing common interests, and pointing out how the group will be damaged if you don't reconcile your differences. Make sure that your motive for speaking is harmonious with the group goals. If you are committed to the group goals, you must be willing to risk criticism and even argument because you believe both can be useful in moving the group toward its objectives.

4. **I am going to present my message in an understandable manner.** You can do this by documenting your ideas; adapting those ideas to your listeners; being willing to answer questions, define terms, and give examples; and cooperating with listeners to reach common meaning. The primary reason for your membership in the group is to work together to share ideas. Remember to keep this in mind as you choose your language and nonverbal communication.

5. **I am willing to continue the dialogue until our ideas are clear, because I value our future interaction.** You can choose to demonstrate a willingness to cooperate, offer to exchange concerns, and agree to consider issues other members raise. You must be prepared to continue to talk. Questions like "Was I clear?" "What do you think about this interpretation?" and "Do you have any questions?" indicate that you are willing to keep talking until your thoughts are clear.

These five principles of rhetorical sensitivity are good standards against which to examine your participation. A person regarded as rhetorically sensitive expresses affiliation with the group and its goal, as well as demonstrating personal integrity.

PERCEPTION

At the most basic level, we can define perception as assigning meaning to stimuli. We look at and listen to other group members, and we make judgments about what we see and hear. When a group member suggests doing things in a certain way at the first meeting, our perception will vary depending on the meaning we assign to that verbal message. We may perceive her to be bossy. We may perceive her to be task oriented and helpful. What contributes to these perceptions? Often our backgrounds and previous communication experiences shape how we perceive messages. Let's say you grew up with a bossy older sister who

Research Check

As the world gets smaller, rhetorical sensitivity becomes even more important. You cannot base your communication solely on the norms of your own culture. "As global companies increasingly rely on virtual teams to conduct short- and long-term projects, business students need to be prepared to manage the communication of intercultural teams. Communicating across cultures using technology can be a difficult task. It requires understanding the advantages and limitations of technology and how to build relationships via technology. Virtual team members need to choose an appropriate communication channel for their purposes and be sure to balance distance work with face-to-face communication. Team leaders should encourage open communication and brainstorming, and avoid assignment of blame. Other strategies for success include: (1) develop a network of good relationships built on trust and understanding, (2) show respect for other cultures and languages, and (3) understand how diversity strengthens the team" (Grosse, 2002, p. 22).

was always trying to control you. In that case, when Reisa suggests that the group start by introducing themselves, you immediately get defensive, perceive her as bossy, and get a sense of dislike for her. Regis, on the other hand, has had numerous small group experiences where no one took charge and nothing got done. He perceives Reisa as efficient and task oriented, and he is excited to work with her. The exact same piece of communication is perceived in two completely different ways.

As you work through the perceptual process, particularly in the initial stages of getting to know one another, you will find yourself *attributing meaning* to the communication you experience. It is important to check these attributions if you are going to be an effective group member. It is detrimental to the group if you assign perceptual meaning and then act on those perceptions as though they were facts. We are often wrong in our perceptions of others. Therefore, it is important to reserve judgment and to listen carefully.

Ray is in a group with Lucinda, Bahiya, and Kelly. When the women are talking, Ray looks at his papers or desk. He rarely makes eye contact, and he never makes confirming noises (uh huh, ok, etc.). He also does not nod his head as the others speak. Since the three women tend to encourage conversation with "uh huh" or "ok," and they always look directly at the speaker, they perceive that Ray is not listening to them, and they attribute sexism as the reason for why he does not communicate as they do. Think of some alternative explanations for Ray's behavior. Why is the attribution of "sexism" probably wrong? How would that attribution of meaning harm this group?

If you are unsure that you have interpreted something accurately, you should ask for clarification. Be sure to question with a spirit of curiosity and sincerity rather than an accusatory tone. Note the difference between the following communication choices based on the box above:

"What IS your problem?"

"What's up with you, Ray? You never listen to us!"

"Ray, are you listening?"

"Hey Ray, when I don't get nonverbal feedback, I feel like you aren't listening—is that the case?"

What is Ray's response likely to be for each of these statements? When he says, "Ya, I'm listening" to the third question, will the problem be fixed? Which statement leads to Ray becoming defensive? Which one gives him the opportunity to describe his listening style? Can you think of a more natural way to ask the last question?

VERBAL COMMUNICATION

Human communication is a complex process. It involves two or more people speaking and listening for good reasons. Because communication is sharing meaning, it is more than just talking. To be effective, communication is audience centered—making sure that each party in the interaction understands.

Research Check

Think about your own orientation. Do you like to talk? Monopolize conversation? How interested are you in what others have to say?

"Our results indicated that men in male-dominated groups exhibited higher levels of power displays, in the form of verbal interruptions, compared with women in female-dominated groups" (Karakowsky, McBey, & Miller, 2004, p. 429).

To be effective as a communicator, you must phrase your ideas so that listeners can understand. One effective means of communicating is to explain how the group will benefit from what you advocate. You may only want them to take note of a particular fact, or you may want them to change their attitude about something. You may want them to take some action. Your responsibility is to make sure your listeners understand what you want and why you feel they should cooperate with you. Gaining the attention of the group is more likely when they can see a mutual benefit.

Once you decide what the goal of your communication is, you can prepare statements in the following categories:

- You may make *categorical statements*: "The facts are. . . ." "The way I see it is. . . ." "I believe that. . . ."
- You may make *process statements*: "I think we agree that. . . ." "Aren't we ready to move to the next point?" "The definition appears complete to me."
- You may make *critical statements*: "I don't think that description of the facts is quite complete. May I add. . . ." "Are we all sure the authority who was just quoted is unbiased?" "Seems to me there were some flaws in the research on which that study was based."
- You may *question*: "Do you believe that for the same reasons he does?" "What evidence does he offer for his position?" "If we added this idea, would you still support the solution?"
- You may *argue*: "I believe that . . . for the following reasons . . . and I do not think that . . . is correct because. . . ."
- You may *reason*: "If this is so, then we are obligated to take either this or that, but if that is flawed, then this is our only alternative despite its limitations."

You'll notice that many of these examples are phrased as *I messages*. These messages enable communicators to state their personal needs or thoughts clearly in a non-accusatory manner. The example above for a critical statement does not read, "That is stupid," which would be inflammatory and a personal attack. Instead it frames the response in terms of what the speaker is thinking. The example for an argument doesn't begin with "Anyone with half a brain would agree. . . ." Instead, they are both framed as "I" messages. They indicate the communication is owned by the speaker.

> Think carefully about how many accusatory remarks you make in daily speech. How often do you frame your communication in "I" statements?

As you select your words, remember that language is *ambiguous*. Meanings are in people, not in the words. When listeners try to understand a message, they may reach a different meaning from what was intended. For instance, if a group member tells you that she had a big breakfast, what does "big" mean? For people who don't eat breakfast, "big" might translate as coffee, juice, and toast. For someone who eats more, "big" might mean bacon, eggs, sausage, and pancakes. As you listen to messages, be aware that you hear the words and interpret them according to your definitions and experiences—which may or may not match those of the speaker. Ask questions and be sure to clarify meanings. When speaking yourself, be as concrete and specific as possible when you choose your words.

How does your group define "having a lot of money," "a long way to drive on vacation," "watching a lot of TV," or "a really hot day"? Why are there differences in your answers?

The following sample group conversations highlight language ambiguity and suggest a rhetorically sensitive approach.

Insensitive: "I think the problem is worded all wrong."

Sensitive: "The statement 'How can we prevent students from doing vandalism in schools?' targets a particular population. With that wording, I think we rule out the chance that vandals might not be students at the school. I suggest we reword the question as 'How can we detect who school vandals are and what steps are necessary for prevention?'"

OR

"The current wording seems to contain a conclusion in the question. Why not 'How can we prevent vandalism in the schools?' That wording will make us find out who the vandals are, and we won't indict all young people right at the start."

The two sensitive choices are specific rather than ambiguous. Note also that these two statements raise objections and offer reasons for those objections. The reasons are not phrased in personal terms; they present reasons other members of the group might respect. In discussion, each participant must talk enough to explain reasons for every statement. Nothing can be taken for granted. We are not encouraging unnecessary wordiness, but be prepared for questions. All group members have beliefs and feelings just as you do. You cannot expect them to agree simply because you think you are right. Be prepared to be specific in your comments.

Your remarks must also reflect a respectful and cooperative tone. In the recommended statements above, the speakers use tact and diplomacy. Personal attacks destroy the underlying base of cooperation that discussion requires. Talk should be about the ideas, not about the people who offer them. For example:

Insensitive: "You've got to be kidding. Only a person who doesn't know the facts would say that the students weren't vandals."

Sensitive: "I never thought that there might be anyone other than kids who vandalize schools. Do we have any evidence about this?"

OR

> "If that's so, then we need to word our question to allow for that possibility. My evidence tells me that students do most of it, but it can't hurt to allow for the possibility that others are involved."

Because communication is an interpretive process, none of us can control completely how others see us. They may get upset by what we say or do, or they may like us in spite of what we say or do. Since we can control only our minds and our mouths, the best we can do is make intelligent guesses about the possible effects of our actions and think about what we say and how we say it. By thinking carefully about our audience as we choose our words, we are being rhetorically sensitive. We also need to clarify with our group members if they say something that we perceive to be insensitive. Perhaps we attributed meaning incorrectly. All it takes is a properly worded, non-confrontational question to elicit feedback.

ACTIVE LISTENING

In discussion groups, listening is vitally important. You will need to consider the ideas as they are presented and to determine if you understood them. After careful consideration, decide whether you need to reply and, if so, what your message will be. There are two mistakes that you should avoid as a good listener.

Potential Problems

First, don't make the mistake of believing that we all have the same meanings for the same words. Remember our discussion of language ambiguity, perception, and attributed meaning? Sometimes we react to speakers in a hostile way if we misunderstand the words. For example, Tricia tells Bill that she thinks he is trendy. She means this as a sincere compliment meaning that Bill is "up and coming" and "on top of things." Bill, who greatly values his independent thinking, is deeply offended. He believes that Tricia just said that he follows the crowd without thinking on his own. This is just one example of how two people understand the same word differently.

Because meanings are in people rather than in words, it is important to check the speaker's intended meaning by giving your interpretation of what was said or by asking questions to pinpoint what was meant. Instead of blowing up, Bill could simply say, "I'm not sure what you mean by that" or "Are you saying that I am following the crowd?" This gives the speaker and listener a chance to clear up the misunderstanding before the wrong meaning causes damage.

Second, don't make the mistake of assuming that people who disagree with you have less sound reasons for their beliefs than you do. Ask why the speaker believes what he or she says. Encourage the speaker to offer justification from his or her point of view. After all, discussion is supposed to reconcile conflicting positions, and you can't reconcile differences until they have been expressed and understood. Active listening includes careful attention to the reasons behind statements. Ask for clarification if you aren't confident that you have interpreted the speaker's intentions. Decide whether the position is supported by good reasons, even if it does not match your point of view.

Content and Relationship Level of Meaning

With those two potential mistakes in mind, let's examine levels of meaning and the six listening/feedback styles. There are two basic levels of meaning of which group members should be aware: *content level* and *relationship level of meaning*. Content level of meaning is the factual interpretation of the words. Relationship level of meaning is the implied or hidden meaning that comes through the tone or wording of the message. In small groups, confusion about levels of meaning might happen in different instances. Jeff says to the group, "Ya, that's a great idea." The content level is simply what the words mean—the idea is great. The relationship level of meaning may be communicated by the emphasis Jeff places on the word "that's." Depending on his paralanguage (the tone in his voice), he might actually be trying to convey that he is disgusted with the idea. By emphasizing the word "that's" in a sarcastic manner, he reveals his opinion that it is a poor idea. Problems will occur if the group reacts to Jeff at the content level, continuing on as if he concurred that the idea is a good one. So we need to be adept at deciphering the relationship level of meaning.

However, we also need to speak clearly and not try to hide behind relationship levels of meaning. Imagine that Rachelle proposes an idea to the group. She thinks it is a terrific idea, and she is very proud of it. The group reacts differently though and finds numerous flaws. Rachelle grows silent. One of the group members notices her behavior and decides to check the perception that Rachelle might be angry. She says, "Rachelle, are you upset that we have dissected your idea?" Rachelle responds "No" in an extremely cynical tone. She wants to get across that she is indeed mad without saying the words, "Yes, I'm really upset that you don't agree." Rachelle is expecting her group members to figure out that she is communicating at the relationship level of meaning. Unfortunately, her group members do not. You may not understand people who do this. Why wouldn't Rachelle just come out and speak plainly? It may have something to do with the fact that she was brought up in family where she was not supposed to "rock the boat" or get angry. She was supposed to make sure everyone else was ok. And she was not encouraged to express feelings of anger. Therefore, she finds it difficult to come out and tell people that she is mad. Instead, she wants them to figure it out.

How effective is Rachelle's communication choice? Can she change her skills at this point in her life? How? Why do many people feel that it is not ok to tell others that they are angry?

Listening/Feedback Styles

Listening in a group takes on many forms. As you work on your skills to decipher language ambiguity, prevent yourself from jumping to conclusions, and learn to interpret content and relationship levels of meaning, you will also want to add the following information on listening/feedback styles to your repertoire of knowledge. The six listening styles are judgmental, directive, empathetic, questioning, interpreting, and active. Some people rely on only one style (think of a judgmental parent who always criticizes). The best communicators, however, are people who can use each of the following styles in the appropriate situation.

It is easiest to understand the styles through examples. Recently a committee of the department chairs of a mid-sized company met and developed a proposal for employees to have a "dress casually on Fridays" policy. They developed this proposal after an extensive problem-solving discussion to generate a solution to the low morale problem at the company. They careful addressed all the steps of problem solving and their proposal was articulate and compelling. However, when they presented it to the administration, the proposal was vetoed immediately with little rationale for the decision. When the department chair group learns about the rejection, they become angry. Jorge says, "I can't believe that they vetoed the proposal. No wonder morale is so low. They don't care about us at all. They just want to control everything. They are micromanagers! Why did we even bother? I hate this place."

Look at the possible listening/feedback styles, imagine another group member making the statement, and think about the pros and cons of each one for this particular situation.

Judgmental listening/feedback means a listener makes a judgment about both the content and the speaker. "Well I told you this was a waste of time." This response makes the speaker sound superior. They knew it all along.

Directive listening/feedback means a listener tells the speaker what to do. "You need to call headquarters and set up an appointment. Go right over their heads. It is time we fought for what is right." This speaker tries to solve the problem by giving advice.

Empathetic listening/feedback means a listener gives he speaker an emotional form of support. "Oh Jorge, I'm really sorry. We all worked so hard. This is such a disappointment."

Questioning is another listening/feedback style. The listener asks probing questions that are not necessarily supportive. "Why didn't you ask to present the solution to them personally?" While this speaker is inviting more conversation, she is also placing a confrontational edge on the communication by implying that Jorge did something wrong.

The *Interpreting* style of listening/feedback means a listener tries to offer another explanation of what happened. This style can be useful in helping the speaker to think of other possible explanations for an event or a better analysis of the problem. "Maybe our reasoning wasn't articulated clearly enough for them to see the connection between morale and casual dress Friday" or "Maybe they are concerned about the image the company would have if clients happened to drop in on Fridays." This listener helps explore other possibilities.

Active listening/feedback means a listener offers supportive questions and makes it clear that he/she is willing to listen. The listener tries to encourage the speaker to continue talking. "So Jorge, what frustrates you most at this point?" or "So Jorge, what do you think we ought to do next?" or "Should we all sit down and discuss possible actions?" Active listening helps the speaker emotionally and/or rationally process his/her reaction to a situation. It doesn't dictate a plan.

NONVERBAL COMMUNICATION

When most people think of communication, they typically think of words. Words, however, comprise a very small portion of our communication. A large part of what we communicate comes from nonverbal communication (all of the communication that is not verbal). Because most of what we send nonverbally is unintentional, we often don't realize that group members interpret our words in light of our nonverbal communication. While there is much more to nonverbal communication, we will focus on only four behaviors that are especially pertinent to group discussion: interaction cues, spatial networks, seating positions, and physical setting.

Interaction Cues

In group discussions, our nonverbal behaviors provide many cues for interactions: facial gestures, physical position, eye contact, and tone of voice indicate our attitudes toward others, feelings, and levels of interest. For example, if Bia turns away or looks aside when someone is speaking, her action may suggest boredom. Conversely, when Rowan sits erect, faces the speaker and maintains direct eye contact, he indicates attentiveness. Although neither interpretation is necessarily accurate, meaning can be derived from each action. Typically, listeners will regard nonverbal messages as more powerful than verbal messages in drawing inferences about the speaker's meaning. Speakers base their conclusions about listener attitudes on what they see listeners doing.

Nonverbal behaviors also regulate or control the flow of discussion. In problem solving, nonverbal cues are the primary method of informally coordinating the flow of the conversation. Typical turn-taking cues include use of eye contact and body posture. It is possible to use turn-taking cues to invite quiet members into discussion and to discourage overly talkative ones from dominating. Someone who is speaking and intends to keep speaking does not sustain eye contact with other members. The interactional cues provided by nonverbal behaviors are a subtle yet very important part of the ongoing communication process in groups.

Be aware of any inappropriate nonverbals you may use on a regular basis. Rolling your eyes, huffing under your breath, and crossed arms are all nonverbals that suggest contempt. A whining tone when you speak sends additional messages along with your content. What will you say to the people in your group who exhibit these nonverbals on a regular basis?

Spatial Networks

The spatial network of the group refers to the overall seating arrangement. There are two basic types of networks: *centralized*, in which one person occupies a central position, and *decentralized*, in which all members have equally prominent spots. In a centralized arrangement, communication flows through one person whose central position makes him or her powerful. Sometimes in classroom groups, the leader will sit on a desk to be higher than the rest of the group. This can help to control the discussion. More than likely your instructor stands at the front of the room in most lectures. Do they look less powerful when they sit down in front? In decentralized patterns, participants have an equal opportunity for face-to-face discussion with other members, rather than having the focus on the leader.

> Think about groups where you have experienced these patterns. Which pattern leads to more balanced participation and greater satisfaction among members? Which promotes careful consideration and deliberation? Have you ever encountered a situation where someone other than the leader tried to occupy a centralized position? What is the reaction of your professor when entering the classroom to find a student in front of the audience?

Seating Positions

Where group members choose to sit will affect how the group works. It appears that whoever occupies a central position exerts more power than those in peripheral positions. People on the physical edges of a group may feel they are not a part of the group, and their participation may wane. Physical constraints in the meeting room can make a decentralized arrangement impossible (as in most board rooms). You can change seating positions at each meeting to give everyone a fair chance to be central. Be aware of the problems of seating conversational people next to one another. If you have more dominant communicators, you want to spread them around the room so that the more quiet members are not on the perimeter where they can easily be excluded.

Physical Setting

The physical setting can influence both the tone of deliberation and patterns of interaction. Relaxed settings such as apartments or homes tend to promote social talk and digression. In addition, casual settings often feature comfortable furniture that encourages people to unwind and take it easy. More formal settings, such as meeting rooms, tend to emphasize one central person and may help to keep an unfocused group on track.

Which setting is better? It all depends on your goals for the group at a particular time. A relaxed environment may be ideal for an initial meeting when members need to get acquainted and become comfortable with one another; however, such a setting might undermine the group later on when key requirements include efficiency and tight, probing analysis. Conference rooms, and even classrooms, offer such useful items as tables for writing, blackboards, and uncomfortable chairs that discourage lingering conversation. Even meeting times can influence interaction. Consider the difference in enthusiasm (and perhaps in attendance) that you could reasonably expect at an 8:00 AM versus a 3:00 PM meeting.

> Keep in mind the cultural differences in nonverbal communication. One of the authors found that when teaching at a northern university, students often met at 9:00 or 10:00 PM for group projects. But at a southern university this was completely unheard of because students at that school believed that anytime after 9:00 PM was "family time."

INDIVIDUAL PREPARATION

Your preparation for group meetings is also an important choice. To do your best in discussion, you must know the topic and the procedure, understand the other members, possess a feeling of compatibility with the leader, and have awareness and understanding of the group goal.

The prepared participant comes ready to present both information and opinions. Effective members review their notes and know what they believe or what reactions would be reasonable. They remember what happened at the last meeting so they do not waste time by asking questions already answered or raising issues that were disposed of previously.

TROUBLESHOOTING

Even with the best of intentions, groups sometimes have bad member relations. As you make your choices, be sure to base them on facts rather than inferences. You have probably learned in other classes/situations that facts are things that we observe and an inference is an assumption that we make about that fact. Sometimes we infer correctly, but other times we are not so successful. It is a fact that Jerri just rolled her eyes at Jim. He saw her do it. Let's say that Jim infers that Jerri doesn't like his idea, and that she is rude. If he continues to make communication choices (such as acting aloof and cool) based on that inference, Jim and Jerri will fall into a downward spiral of interaction and eventually stop talking to each other. However, there may be alternative explanations. It may be that Jerri was daydreaming about something that happened earlier in the day and the nonverbal eye movement was related to that. It could be that she had something in her eye. There are multiple reasons why people do things and say things. So, how can you avoid making mistakes? Ask questions! Check your inferences! Something as simple as Jim asking, "Jerri, do you find something wrong with what I just said?" can immediately clarify a mistaken inference.

Remember, as you make your individual choices, each and every one will affect the way that the system functions. If you make a mistake and offend or upset someone, apologize. While you should always speak your mind and feel comfortable with being critical of ideas, you need to do so in a rhetorically-sensitive manner.

�౭ 5 ౭

Making Effective Choices When Leading

Every member needs to be concerned with group leadership; the leader directly affects the group's ability to achieve its goals. All members should be prepared to move into the leadership position if the group needs them. There may be times when a leader is absent due to other commitments or an illness; he or she may also deliberately miss a meeting in order to avoid influencing the group (as in the case of groupthink).

This chapter will increase your understanding of how to lead. It will also give you a sound basis for judging how well others are leading. Armed with this information, you will be able to assist leaders when necessary.

SELECTING AND SHAPING A LEADER

Your group can use one of three possible options for setting up the group:

- Designate one person as leader
- Take a chance that a leader will emerge
- Hope that all leadership functions will be divided among the various members and no power conflicts will erupt

Designating a leader is the safest and most common approach. If your group is part of a larger organization, a leader was probably designated when the group was established. If the designation is up to your group, you have some choices. You can ask for volunteers; you can see who has the most experience and select that person; you can vote on a leader. Keep in mind, though, that a person who is not willing to lead is generally not a good choice.

57

The second option, hoping a leader will emerge, is a serious gamble. If one doesn't emerge, the group may falter. Even worse, two members seeking leadership may make rivalry the dominant issue, thus distracting everyone from the task. Members who emerge as leaders sometimes lack sufficient experience. Just because someone is dominant does not mean that they have leadership skills. If group members do not voice their preference for having a leader, members who have the ability to lead may not do so. Keep in mind, the charging authority may designate a leader who is not equipped to lead. In that group, an emergent leader may eventually take over. In that particular case there will be two leaders—one who has the title, and one who performs the functions.

The third option, assuming that leadership can be distributed effectively among members, is truly risky. When tasks are not completed or are not done well, no one person is ultimately responsible. In addition, there is no central person who is keeping track of what has been completed. If there are power struggles over who should do what, there is no one with the authority to mediate. The group can become divided and purposeless. You would have to look long and hard to find a leaderless administrative committee, board of directors, corporate committee, or other serious problem-solving unit. Specifying a leader and fixing responsibility in one person is generally the wisest procedure.

Once in a while, someone will suggest the idea of co-leaders. While in theory the idea of sharing the workload is a good one, generally co-leaders are suggested when no one wants the leadership responsibility. In this situation you end up with two people in the position that no one wanted. Unless co-leaders are highly motivated, detail-oriented people who like working with one another, the only benefit to having co-leaders is that they each have someone else to blame when the leadership functions are not performed.

However, not everyone believes that single leaders are advisable. Advocates of leaderless discussion (in which all members are expected to perform leadership tasks) argue that discussion should be a cooperative venture in which all group members participate equally. They claim that a leaderless group can be as effective as one operating under a single leader. The operative word is "can." A leaderless group can be effective—if all members participate with a spirit of goodwill and are very considerate of one another. This kind of utopian situation is rare. Furthermore, if there is any conflict in the group, it is virtually impossible for a leaderless group to resolve it. Certainly, a group with a designated leader can also be ineffective if the leader is incompetent or conflicts are irreconcilable, but it is easier to replace a leader than it is to train people to get along so well that they do not need one.

Advocates of leaderless groups also suggest that shared leadership facilitates democracy and that a single leader can lead to authoritarian control. There is no necessary connection between individual leadership

How will your group decide who should be the leader? What criteria will you use for your selection? What should your group do if no one wants to be the leader?

and authoritarianism. When a leader is authoritarian, it is because members have encouraged him or her to assume primary control of the group. Members tend to reinforce the leadership style they want. Often this is unintentional, as are many of the choices humans make. If, however, the communicative behaviors in the group reinforce a controlling leader, group members have chosen the style of leadership they receive.

One way to exercise control of leadership behaviors is through role negotiation in which a leader and members tell each other what is expected and why. You can think of this as a contract between a leader and members, where both parties have control over the details of the contract. While there are many theories of effective leadership, we believe in an adaptive approach to leadership for small-group problem-solving situations. Unlike other views of leadership, the adaptive approach regards leading as a highly dynamic, changing process. The adaptive approach means that there is no recipe for a perfect leader. Every group is different. To be effective, a leader must respond to the needs of the members in the group and to the situation. The assumption is that effective leadership stems from adapting to particular circumstances, members, and tasks and to changes in all these aspects of problem solving.

In developing the contract between the leader and the group members, a group should discuss its desires for all aspects of leading. Members may specify that they want a leader to enforce a schedule, design a schedule, or work with members to develop a schedule. They may ask a leader to assign tasks to members or specify that members cannot be pressed into service without their consent. The group may request that a leader run meetings formally, informally, or delegate running meetings to another member, and so on. The leader can also voice how he or she envisions the job of leader, share his or her strengths and weaknesses, and tell the group what he or she might be comfortable and uncomfortable doing. Reasonable people can usually work out a set of agreements acceptable to all and constructive for the group objectives.

By negotiating the nature of leadership as well as its limitations, members can avoid authoritarian control. They can reap the substantial benefits of having a central person charged with defined functions who will assist the group in doing its work with maximum efficiency and quality. Be sure that your group records its decisions on leader responsibilities in your minutes. That way you have a written record that you can refer to if difficulties should arise later.

Research Check

"Democratic leadership results in more satisfied group members than autocratic leadership. . . . It appears that people in groups do not prefer to be subjected to domineering or manipulative leadership but instead are more satisfied when they are allowed to participate in group decisions" (Foels, Driskell, Mullen, & Salas, 2000, p. 692).

One of the important elements of the standard agenda is that it compels both group members and the leader to engage in reflective consideration of what they have done and what they need to do. Emphasis on personal responsibility facilitates getting the work accomplished. When members believe that what they do makes a difference, they are less likely to concede power to an authoritarian leader.

REMAINING EFFECTIVE AS A LEADER

In order to remain effective, a leader must stay in tune with the group's needs and meet their expectations. An agreement on roles is a good start, but subsequently the leader must analyze the members and the situation, inspire commitment, and stay alert to changing requirements.

Member Needs

Leaders need to be aware of their personal skills and weaknesses as well as their potential impact on others. To analyze members, leaders must first realize that there is great diversity in what people want in a leader. Although many people like to be guided by a democratic leader who works with them, others prefer a directive leader who takes charge and even cracks the whip occasionally. The democratic style will not work well with followers who crave direction, and the authoritarian style will fail with followers who have initiative and the experience to back it up. William Jurma (1979) found that people who are not highly organized prefer a leader who provides structure for them, while well-organized individuals do not appreciate so much direction. Leaders need to adapt their actions not just to the group as a whole, but also to the needs and preferences of individual members—a challenging task.

Be sure that you understand what the members want from you as the leader. Be honest in what you can and cannot supply. Some members will desire tight authority, while others will appreciate greater independence. Some groups expect a leader to fulfill a strong procedural role, while other groups seek task or climate roles from their leaders. If the group members want someone to organize the agenda and plan for all of the details but you are not a detail-oriented person, it might be wise to reconsider the leadership role. In another example, the group members might want a leader who is good at conflict resolution because there are members of the group who do not get along. If you are a detail-oriented person but have no skill at resolving arguments, then this job is not for you. If the thought of being the leader of the group is exciting to you because you love to "be in charge," "tell people what to do," or "have members' undivided attention," then you may want to consider a career in the armed forces rather than a position as a discussion leader.

Have a conversation about leadership with your group members. Don't assume you know what they need. A good leader focuses on how to help group members excel. Leading is about the members, not about you.

Situations

To remain effective, leaders also need to analyze and adapt to their particular situations. The leader must recognize competition confronting the group and be sensitive to time pressures. If a deadline is approaching, the style of leading may change. In that situation, a leader might become more directive in order to assure that tasks are completed. The leader should be aware of the strengths and weaknesses of the group and of its members and should monitor role and status development among members. For example, if a group has suffered a recent defeat, the leader may need to give a pep talk and provide a lot of support as members start a new task. On the other hand, if the group has had a recent success, the leader should be wary of the dangers of overconfidence and of excessive cohesion, which could interfere with constructive conflict in deliberations. In short, a leader needs to have a sense of the potential of the group. Careful, informed thought about the group and its members is a leader's basic tool.

Inspiring Commitment

Persuading each member to be as committed and effective as possible represents another challenge of leadership. The leader of a small group can develop a personal relationship with each member—being inspirational to one person, collaborative with another, and directive with a third. By meeting each member's needs, the members will be more satisfied with the group experience and will perform more effectively. To assume that there is a cookie-cutter mold for dispensing leadership that you can stamp on each person in the same way is a costly mistake.

Behavioral Flexibility

Analysis of members and situations informs a leader of what is needed to make a group work smoothly. The next step is to provide what she or he has diagnosed. Effective leaders have mastered a wide repertoire of behaviors, and they know how and when to employ each. Here are two examples that demonstrate the kind of flexibility we are talking about.

First, there is the case of Samantha, a student in a small group who was selected as the leader. At an early meeting of her group, she assumed a very casual demeanor. She encouraged members to talk, allowed minor tangents to punctuate discussion, and often solicited members' advice on directions that the group should pursue. She appeared to be a classic democratic leader. As the going got rougher and the deadlines for a report got nearer, however, Samantha tightened the reins. She gradually increased the amount of direction she imposed, diplomatically but force-fully curbed digressions, and assigned specific subcommittee tasks to members. The group moved along efficiently and effectively, turning out a report that earned high marks for all from the instructor.

Samantha knew what she was doing each step of the way. In initial meetings, her goals were to build a sense of team spirit and to gain insight into how each member operated without any direction from her. As soon as she had a handle on the group's tendencies and the inclina-tions of individual members, she could define her own role appropriately. By the time the group had to accelerate its efforts, she had earned mem-bers' confidence, so they accepted the pressure she put on them and fol-lowed the directions she proposed. She analyzed her situation and did what was necessary to lead the group to success.

A second example is the case of Brent, who moved into a junior man-agement position in a manufacturing company. He had studied human relations in college and had been taught that participatory decision mak-ing was desirable. Brent's first assignment was to chair a committee charged with reviewing the executive training program and recommend-ing methods for improving it. Brent applied what he had learned by working on an equal-to-equal basis with the members who held posi-tions similar to his in the company. The report was a success.

A little later Brent was asked to head a committee of factory workers charged with recommending ways to increase production. Brent tried to run this group just as he had run the previous one. He treated the factory workers just as he had treated his executive colleagues. He encouraged everyone to participate, but the workers did not respond to his efforts. He might have failed completely had the union representative not offered some advice. The representative told Brent that the workers were natu-rally distrustful of management and specifically suspicious of an execu-tive who "pretended" to see them as equals. They thought Brent was patronizing them, trying to win their confidence in order to determine whether they were loyal to the company. Brent considered this advice and modified his leadership accordingly. He organized agendas and told the members what he needed from them; he asked specific questions about each department in the company and assigned the members to gather specific data; he set and enforced deadlines. After a few meetings under this revised leadership, the workers began to respond to Brent's style and to produce good ideas. The final report was thorough and sound.

As these two cases illustrate, a leader's job is to figure out what needs to be done to realize the potential within a specific group of people working on a particular task. To find out what is needed, a leader must be flexible enough to alter his or her communicative behaviors to fit the requirements.

Overall, there appear to be a few expectations of leaders common to most group situations. Generally, leaders are expected:

- To provide some basic organization for the problem-solving process by managing an agenda acceptable to members.

- To summarize deliberations, particularly at points of transition from one agenda item to another.

- To indicate connections among issues discussed at different times by suggesting causes and consequences of decisions.

- To ensure that conflict does not impede the work of the group by discovering and using ways and means of resolving conflicts between members.

- To test for consensus before moving the group along and to record agreements once made.

- To delegate responsibilities for record keeping, logistics, research, and so on, to members, and to supervise members to be sure assigned tasks are completed.

These basic responsibilities are associated with leadership in most contexts. Beyond these few common responsibilities, generalizations about the requirements of leadership are risky. Each group situation is unique and has unique needs and opportunities.

Research Check

"Group leadership from a bona fide group theory perspective was examined. Twenty-three effective group leaders were interviewed in depth about what they believe is important in leading groups. Five themes emerged: (a) establishing the intention for the overall project; (b) building the team and developing a positive group culture; (c) monitoring and managing the team's interaction; (d) managing the group's task and keeping the group focused; and (e) communication behaviors and personal characteristics of the leader. Effective group leaders take group leadership seriously and work at improving their performance and exhibit self-monitoring and adaptive behaviors" (Galanes, 2003, p. 741).

PREPARING FOR LEADERSHIP

We've just noted that leaders are regarded as more responsible than others for what a group accomplishes or fails to accomplish. Because leaders have special responsibilities for group outcomes, they need to prepare carefully in the following four areas.

- Organizing the agenda.
- Analyzing the group and individual members.
- Controlling the physical situation.
- Planning personal style.

These things take a lot of time, so you should not agree to hold a leadership position unless you can devote the time necessary to do it well.

The Agenda

An effective leader understands the issues that must be discussed and will organize them in a way that facilitates group progress. Leaders who have solid overviews of the task and who distribute a logical agenda to the group usually provide effective guidance.

Competent leaders often prepare two outlines: one that is private and one that is distributed to members. The private outline identifies key issues and the leader's questions or concerns about each. Specific questions or comments may be noted and potential resources may be penciled in. The second outline, known as the *public agenda,* is for members and should be distributed in advance. The purpose of the public agenda is to inform members of what will be covered at a particular meeting so that they can prepare for productive, informed discussion. Leaders who distribute public agendas in advance of meetings close the door for excuses: "I didn't know we were going to work on that tonight, so I'm not prepared to report."

The public agenda need not be lengthy; its purpose is to inform all members of the topics that will be covered. Here, for example, is a public agenda for an initial group meeting:

Agenda for the Opening Meeting

Please come prepared to discuss these items at the opening meeting at 4:00 PM on Monday, November 12, in 107 Memorial Hall.

1. Why was this group set up?
2. What are we charged to produce or do and for whom?
3. How were the members of this group selected? Do we have special talents, experiences, etc., pertinent to the task?
4. How do we want to run this group? What do you expect from me as the leader? What kind of schedule is reasonable for meeting dates and times?

Members who receive an agenda like this are more likely to come prepared for productive discussion. A basic agenda format is also available in chapter 2.

The Group and Its Members

Let's look more closely at some of the basic understandings a leader needs to acquire in order to adapt to group members. First, a leader will want to know why members volunteered or were appointed to the group. When members are volunteers, a leader may assume they are interested; but they may not be fully informed, and they are likely to be biased. People who volunteer to work on tasks usually have some preconceived idea about the right solution. Since volunteers can walk away at anytime, leaders need to analyze carefully how to manage a volunteer situation.

When working with appointed members, a leader should figure out what issues are at stake and how each member's involvement can be secured. Also, the leader may need to provide greater background information on the issues to people who are appointed because they may have limited knowledge of the problem.

Astute leaders attempt to discern the personal qualities of individual members. Careful observation of members during early meetings should help a leader recognize particular talents and problems (remember Samantha's strategy?). The leader can then use these insights to help each member become as comfortable and effective as possible. Individuals with obvious communication skills may be the group's primary interviewers; articulate members may be asked to represent the group to outsiders; those with a flair for detail may be assigned to work on data collection and analysis, and so forth. The goal is to find ways to realize each member's potential for constructive contribution to the group goal.

There is cause for caution, however. A leader must be certain to distribute the load equally. Sometimes a leader will assign a majority of tasks to a particularly competent member. While this might seem to be a good way to assure that the work will be done well, the member who is overburdened may become resentful or burned out, resulting in less work or a bad attitude in the future. We knew a young woman who worked with a non-profit organization. She impressed the people in charge with her strong attention to detail, innovative ideas, and ability to facilitate group process; others in the group were incompetent. As time went on, she was the only one who was asked to do anything in the group, because the leader knew she would do it well. She eventually resigned because she resented having to shoulder all the responsibility. If the other members would have learned from her skills and taken part of the workload, she might have stayed much longer.

A leader needs to be prepared to address members who are not doing their work. It is always unpleasant to have those discussions, but the responsibility in this case does fall to the leader. If your leader is unwilling to deal with conflict situations that affect the group, then he or she is not worthy of the title.

In addition to personal qualities, the leader can spot behavioral tendencies in members through observation and find ways to manage them. For example, the leader may want to calm those who tend to dominate discussion and encourage those who tend to withdraw. If a normally productive member seems ill at ease or uninvolved, the leader may want to call that person aside to find out whether there are problems external to the group that are affecting the member's participation. A member experiencing job strain or personal crisis may be unable to contribute much to the group at the moment, but a leader who gives support and understanding preserves the possibility of future contributions from that individual.

Another behavioral tendency to withdraw might result from the group rejecting someone's idea. The leader may need to support that person in other areas or work with that person to revise the idea before the group meets again. Sometimes people have a predisposition to argue heatedly. It is not wise to let hostilities fester. If two members engage in a heated argument, it may be important for the leader to do some informal checking on whether there is any residual animosity. Dropping in on each of the two or going out for coffee with each may allow the leader to smooth any ruffled feathers and preserve good relations in the group.

A problem-solving group is composed of individuals with special personalities, skills, deficiencies, and self-images. The leader's primary responsibility is to help each member find ways of being effective and valuable to the group. Leaders who invest the time and thought required to understand individual members empower them to contribute. The group reaps the reward of seeing a collection of diverse individuals working together as a smoothly functioning unit.

The Physical Situation

While the physical situation in which a group meets is less important than task and interpersonal issues, it is still an important aspect of planning. The leader should attempt to make the physical setting conducive to effective problem solving. The leader should consider furniture, facilities, and supplies.

Decentralized arrangement of furniture is usually a good choice because it allows all members to interact. The leader should think about whether the group needs comfortable seating (overstuffed chairs, for example) or a more formal table and chairs. Do the group members need to be relaxed and engaged in discussion? Do they need to take notes? Do they have trouble staying awake? These are important considerations as the leader decides on the setting.

Facilities and equipment are also important. Is the group located near bathrooms? Can they stand up, stretch, and move around? The leader should consider distractions as well. It might make more sense to meet in a library conference room than in someone's dorm or apartment. Phone interruptions and people stopping by will slow a group's progress tremendously. We knew one group that complained of having six- to eight-hour meetings. After careful questioning of this group, it turned out that they would take extended breaks to watch a *World Wrestling Federation* broadcast in the middle of their meetings. Also, groups often use a computer and copier during small-group problem solving. Your computer should be linked to the Internet and to library resources if appropriate. Having the proper facilities and equipment is essential to good group progress.

Supplies are also important. The leader should provide extra paper and pens; group members often arrive without such supplies. Bringing refreshments is also important if the meeting will last more than one hour. A brief break for refreshments often rejuvenates a group and allows them to refocus on the task with renewed energy.

Personal Style

Ultimately, leaders must try to mesh their preferences for leadership style with members' requirements. Without sacrificing personal integrity or values, a leader should be able to accommodate the critical needs of a group and to persuade the group to accommodate him or her on other issues.

Gender can make a difference in personal style as well. People who lead with masculine communication skills tend to be directive whereas people who lead with feminine communication skills tend to be more collaborative.

Research Check

Sabine Koch (2005) reports "the aim of the present research was to demonstrate that EAD [Evaluative Affect Display] in small groups can be one means of communicating prejudice toward female leaders. This effect was shown in Study 1, a replication and extension of the Butler and Geis study (1990), where female leaders received more negative affect display, while at the same time they were rated more competent than male leaders on scales. Yet in Study 2, a field study of real teams in organizational contexts, the effect failed to emerge. Study 2 instead found that all women, and especially women leaders, generally received more affect, positive and negative. Teams led by a woman were much more affectively expressive than were teams led by a man, and all-women teams were the most expressive" (p. 696).

Although not statistically significant, Koch found that "Women in leadership positions received 3 times as many negative affect displays as did men (12 vs. 4)" (p. 692).

STRATEGIES FOR LEADING

Leadership succeeds or fails on accomplishments. Effectiveness in achieving group goals grows out of a leader's action choices, which influence five dimensions of problem solving: members' perceptions of the leader; members' perceptions of each other and of themselves; members' perceptions of the group as whole; members' judgments on substantive issues; and the pace of discussion. True to the systems perspective, these five dimensions interact.

Influencing Members' Perceptions of the Leader

Consciously or unconsciously, leaders influence how members perceive them. The most effective leaders do this at a conscious level in order to control how they appear and thus how they influence others. Leaders who act informally and socialize with members promote perceptions of themselves as relaxed, unassuming, and part of the team. This can be helpful in putting members at ease and in minimizing status differences between leaders and members. It may also be appropriate when an appointed leader first takes charge and wants to show members he or she is relaxed and does not intend to run the whole show. The leader should be careful, however, not to act so informally that it is not possible to tighten up later if the need emerges.

A leader tends to be seen as task oriented and efficient when he or she relies on formal procedures and directive comments. This kind of presentation may be appropriate when time pressures are keen or when a group seems undisciplined. The leader who confines comments to the task and who curbs members from digressive talk generally instills businesslike attitudes in members. The trade-off may be resentment if members really do not want to work on the task and feel they are being forced. Thus, a leader should balance the potential loss of goodwill against the need for group progress.

Through communication, leaders tell members who they are. If you are a leader, contemplate the self-image you present to members and the

---

Research Check

"Certain IM [impression management] tactics used by team leaders may heighten specific aspects of group satisfaction...With regard to Group Cohesion, it was found that Ingratiation and Exemplification increased feelings of cohesiveness within the group. Attempting to present oneself as likable would help team members be attracted to one another, thereby increasing cohesion. Likewise, trying to appear morally worthy by working extra hours and attaining referent power might increase the attractiveness of the team and bring members closer together" (Rozell & Gundersen, 2003, p. 217).

methods by which you achieve it. If you are a member, ask yourself how your leader seems to come across and why. These questions should lead to some intriguing insights.

Influencing Members' Perception of Each Other and of Themselves

Group work is a cooperative enterprise in which each member affects the whole unit. Further, all members are affected by the overall climate of the group, which may encourage or discourage participation. For these reasons, leaders need to think carefully about how they want to influence members' views of themselves and of each other.

A leader who recognizes members heightens their commitment to group goals and their motivation to contribute. Whatever members do for the group deserves acknowledgment, and exceptional contributions merit special praise. Leaders can set an example for mutual supportiveness by being generous with words that call attention to the good work of individuals. Sincere recognition that is distributed among members tends to strengthen a group's sense of pride and to enhance members' respect for themselves and for each other. Of course, leaders should avoid so much praise that it ceases to mean anything. Likewise, leaders should be cautious of lavishing extensive praise on only one or two members, since this might create divisiveness within the group.

The leader can further enhance respect among members by demonstrating interest in what each says. There is no better way to undermine the confidence of individuals than to yawn when they are addressing the group. A leader who is inattentive or appears to be bored tells other members that they need not respect what is being said. Thus, leaders need to choose actions that demonstrate respect. These types of communicative behaviors persuade members to think highly of themselves, each other, and their work as a group.

Leaders' actions influence how members perceive themselves and what they regard as appropriate orientations to group work. Through references to each member's participation, achievements, and skills, a leader contributes to role development in the group. By appointing people to record, present position papers, or report on research, a leader enhances their visibility. Punctuality and attendance are encouraged by leadership actions that censor violations. If members start dragging in late or skipping meetings, the leader should indicate disapproval quickly before members conclude it is acceptable to miss meetings. Norms form quickly, so a leader must act with dispatch. Leaders may ask the group to draft a letter to someone who is absent more than once or may remind a tardy member that the meeting began some time ago and lateness is an insult to everyone who managed to come on time. By putting individuals on the spot, the leader can enforce discipline without resorting to heavy penalties. Also, the leader demonstrates to other members that lateness and absenteeism are not condoned. Remember, the leader is a prime setter of group norms.

Influencing Members' Perceptions of the Group as a Whole

The ways in which members see their group decidedly affects how they participate and what they achieve. Effective leaders work to help members see group goals as important and as the focal point of deliberation. The leader should make every effort to keep members from thinking participation is a means of gaining personal points—an attitude that fosters competitiveness within the unit. The leader should act in ways that promote a team orientation. It is important that leaders avoid singling out particular members for special privilege or harassment.

Persuading members to see the group as talented and able is a primary concern for leaders. A leader should highlight group progress and remind members of any past successes. The leader can also promote the perception of the group as a whole by encouraging themes, slogans, or logos for the group. We generally encourage class groups to come up with a name. One of the groups called themselves "Synergistic Solutions." Their slogan, "working together to bond theory with reality," helped them to see their purpose as a group.

Influencing Members' Judgments on Substantive Issues

Because leaders have the greatest responsibility for a group's results, they need to devote special effort to helping the group move in productive directions and to draw appropriate conclusions. Sometimes members become attached to idealistic plans that have slim chances of working, or they resist coming to a recommendation that violates preconceived biases. At such points, a leader's responsibility is to persuade the group to reexamine decisions, to guard against prejudices, and to be realistic about what can be achieved.

Generally leaders should try to avoid acting as advocates, because they have strong influence over members. Sometimes, however, advocacy is necessary. When it is, the leader should distinguish between personal views and those associated with the positions of leader—for example, "The executive committee will never accept the plan we're discussing. They've turned down every committee proposal that restricts executive privileges. If we want to have any impact on corporate policy, we'll need to find the next best plan." This comment reflects the role of a leader. By contrast, the following is a personal stance, unlikely to win support. "I don't believe in that, and I want an alternative."

Leaders influence how members perceive issues when they design the agenda. By emphasizing certain items on an agenda distributed in advance, leaders demonstrate what issues are central. Leaders may also influence judgments by the ordering of agenda items. By putting several simple matters first, the leader helps the group approach more difficult issues with confidence based on previous success.

Influencing the Pace of the Discussion

Some meetings seem to drag on forever without accomplishing much. On the other hand, most of us have been in discussions that moved so quickly that we felt railroaded into a decision. An effective leader tries to avoid both extremes by encouraging members to work at an efficient pace, neither so fast that they make hasty judgments nor so slow that everyone becomes bored.

The leader can influence the pace of discussion by adding time limits to each agenda item. When there is a great deal of work to be done in a single meeting, it is the leader's responsibility to persuade members that it can be done and to generate a mood of efficiency. By adding time limits to each agenda item, the leader helps members gauge their progress as they move through the agenda and helps the group stay on target.

Leaders sometimes expedite work by wrapping up particular issues. Consider, for example, a leader who needed to complete and submit a written report covering the initial work of the committee. She called a meeting and told members they would be responsible for completing the report during the session and asked the writers of the report to distribute copies to all members in attendance. These actions informed the writers that the leader approved the substance of the report and that the focus of the meeting was to edit it for style. While the members might have preferred to discuss the issues a little longer, the leader knew the report was solid, and she exercised her authority.

To slow the pace of discussion, leaders may interject questions and encourage elaboration of ideas. Sometimes leaders need to calm an enthusiastic group in order to prevent premature settling on issues. The leader may say, "Hang on, Rick. I'm not clear on the details of what you just proposed," or "Just for the sake of the record, let's pin down some of these general points," or "I think this may not be the only possible solution, although it seems to be the only one we've generated. Can any of you help me identify some other options?" Communication of this type sets a tone for questioning and probing. If members are not being critical and careful in their own thinking, the leader must persuade them to be so.

Leaders are persuasive agents who influence their groups in the five dimensions we've just considered. Each action a leader takes or comment he/she makes can affect the climate of the group, the investment of individual members, and the quality of the outcomes that result. The role of a leader builds personal communication skills and can lead to tremendous satisfaction when the group performs well and its task is successfully completed.

❧ 6 ❧

Creating a
Constructive Climate
and Managing Conflict

Conflict is an essential element in group problem solving, but it must be managed appropriately. The procedure for handling conflict can make your group experience positive and effective or negative and ineffective. Members of discussion groups should obviously work to develop a constructive climate from the beginning. If a comfortable tone is established the group will be able to turn serious disagreement into a useful method of discovering the best solutions. The choices about communication behavior detailed in the last chapter are important elements in building a constructive group climate.

ROLE OF CONFLICT IN DISCUSSION

If we told you that you are about to have a conflict, how would you react? Some people would be curious—"Bring it on," they might say. Others would be uncomfortable, because they avoid conflict at all costs. People react differently to conflict, so it is important to make the best choices possible as you navigate through the group process. Many people also have a negative connotation of the word conflict. They tend to think "fighting" or "aggressiveness." Conflict, however, is simply what happens when group members have a disagreement or difference of opinions. Is difference of opinions necessarily a bad thing? Of course not. Disagreeing is good when people are trying to think and solve problems! The main thing is to resolve the conflict in a positive manner.

What do you think of when someone says "conflict"? Define the term and ask two friends what their definitions are. Do your definitions differ? Now ask the friends how they feel about conflict. Do the definitions and feelings match? If you or your friends are uncomfortable with conflict what, specifically, makes you uncomfortable?

We have stated that conflict is essential for good group problem solving. Conflict is an excellent way to examine ideas carefully. Spirited inquisition yields thoughts and ideas that would otherwise never be articulated. Yet, many people avoid conflict or are uncomfortable with the thought of it. The key to productive conflict is that your group manages it effectively. Groups that appropriately manage conflict may find that they produce even more effective solutions. Julia Wood (1977a) identified three distinct values of conflict that merit attention.

1. *Conflict allows a group to entertain diverse ideas.* This in turn helps members gain a broad understanding of the multiple facets of a problem. The first objective of problem-solving discussion is to reach an understanding of the problems you intend to solve. At this stage it is necessary to examine background information carefully. You need to examine diverse ideas about the nature of the charge and background of the problem. One member may see something that others haven't noticed, so it is useful for members to offer alternative interpretations of the task.

2. *Conflict encourages the expression of divergent points of view and thereby provides a group with the potential for a greater number of alternatives from which to select final solutions.* If a group gets tired or apathetic at the solution stage, or if it cannot refrain from the natural tendency to want to grasp the first solution, then it may agree too quickly on a superficially examined solution. Furthermore, if the group has not established conflict as a norm, then members will hesitate to criticize or challenge someone who presents a solution. If the entire problem-solving process ends with one person stating a solution and the rest of the group agreeing, the essence of good, systematic problem solving is lost. Well-reasoned recommendations tend to result from lively deliberations about a number of alternate ideas.

3. *The excitement generated by healthy conflict stimulates interaction and involvement among members.* Constructive conflict focused on issues heightens members' interest and sharpens their participation skills. When differences are welcomed and considered earnestly, each member may feel free to volunteer ideas and to

respond thoughtfully and honestly to those of others. This kind of deliberation can be genuinely interesting. Creativity in discussion seems to thrive on constructive conflict, on the welcoming of differing viewpoints as legitimate, and on the willingness to respond with care and thoroughness to each viewpoint. Without some disagreement to stimulate sharp thinking, discussion can become lethargic and boring.

These conflict roles are vitally important, yet the value is contingent on proper management of conflict. When members do not handle conflict well, its benefits disappear. In fact, negative outcomes are likely. Group members must learn to manage conflict to achieve its potential values.

TYPES OF CONFLICT

Conflict exists on a continuum ranging from purely disruptive to purely constructive. While most instances of conflict fall somewhere between these two opposites, we will confine our analysis to the two extremes: This will give you a perspective on the essential character of ideal conflict management and its counterpart.

$$\longleftarrow \hspace{4cm} \longrightarrow$$
disruptive   **constructive**

Disruptive conflict is characterized by a sense of competition in which members feel they are pitted against one another and only one person or one faction can emerge victorious. Winning becomes more important than achieving common goals. Lost in the disruption is the goal of collective interests in which all members win with the best solution. Some members tend to become so ego-involved with their ideas that any criticism or disagreement is perceived as a personal attack. For example, if Bob believes his idea is the best and refuses to compromise, he halts the effective discussion process. He may get hostile when others point out weaknesses in his position. If he can't "win" he may continue to hold up the process, which inconveniences all of the members.

In disruptive conflict situations, members are likely to feel apprehensive and threatened. Consequently, they become defensive and may act aggressively or withdraw with feelings of resentment. Obviously, if people withdraw, then valuable ideas are lost. If they act aggressively, they may disrupt relationships in the group. Under such conditions, it is nearly impossible for members to consider ideas intelligently. If disruptive conflict is allowed to continue for long, the group may form factions. Team spirit will go out the window—as will any possibility of compromise.

If your group experiences a situation in which two members engage in face-to-face confrontation, it is possible to diffuse the situation. We recommend that you urge them to address their remarks to the group rather than to one another. As the group builds a position from both points of view, the two parties can often build a reconciliation when they see that their ideas are taken seriously. This is the substance of negotiation and compromise.

Research Check

"The results of this study add to the current understanding of the expression of intragroup conflict in FTF [Face to face] and CMC [Computer mediated communication] groups. In summary, the following results were obtained: (a) Initially, CMC groups exhibited more relationship and process conflict than FTF groups, but these differences were not apparent in later stages; and (2) CMC and FTF groups exhibited similar amounts of task conflict at all times" (Hobman, Bordia, Irmer, & Chang, 2002, p. 456).

Constructive conflict develops when members understand they are using disagreement to reach common objectives. Disagreements are managed within the context of collective interests. In constructive conflict situations, members support each other's presentations of ideas, even if they disagree with the content of those ideas.

For instance, if the group sets a constructive climate in the beginning, then the spirit of inquiry is not seen as a threat but rather as a way to make the best decision. Ray presents an idea to the group. Immediately Kristi starts asking questions: Where did the information come from? How much will it cost? Because there is a constructive climate in this group, Ray understands that Kristi is only asking questions to help refine the idea into a usable one for the group. If that constructive climate had not been established, then Ray could become defensive, and destructive conflict might ensue.

Constructive conflict means that we are critically examining ideas and asking questions without attacking other people. An equally important aspect of constructive conflict is that members tend to invite others to critique, question, or modify ideas they present. Discussion stays focused on issues, not personalities, and the channels of communication remain open.

Constructive management of conflict benefits everyone. Members broaden their perspectives on the problem; they generate enough solutions to compare relative merits and identify backup positions; and they become increasingly cohesive because they have engaged in vigorous conflict without dividing the group. Members learn to trust and respect one another when they discover it is possible to talk intelligently and productively about differences of opinion.

Describe a group situation in which you experienced disruptive conflict. How was it resolved? Describe a group situation in which you experienced productive conflict. How was it fostered?

COMPONENTS OF CONSTRUCTIVE CLIMATE

The ideal constructive climate (defined as "interpersonal tone" for the group) features cooperativeness, openness, and rhetorical sensitivity. These qualities are important because they encourage free expression of ideas, consideration for and an understanding of different viewpoints, and an awareness of shared goals that transcend individual positions on particular issues.

Cooperativeness

Communication that emphasizes teamwork lays the foundation for a cooperative orientation. Using terms such as "we," "our," "us," "our committee," and "mutual concerns" fosters a sense of cohesiveness within the group.

Have you been in groups that used team language? Ones that did not? Were those experiences different? In what way?

In addition to language choices to describe the group, you also have choices to use supportive communication within the group. Taking a minute to compliment another group member on an insightful comment or to voice support for a well-reasoned idea indicates that you are interested in the other members and listening. Even if you don't agree, it is possible to be supportive. You might ask for clarification, elaboration, or further support for an idea. It is important to state honestly that you disagree and to invite the other person to work with you to figure out the basis of your disagreement and to find a mutually agreeable position.

To promote cooperative, team orientations, it is generally advisable to minimize authorship of ideas. If Ellen suggested X and Levi proposed Y, avoid comparisons of, "Ellen's position versus Levi's position." That approach is likely to create polarization in the group and may invoke competitiveness between Ellen and Levi. It is better to say, "So, we have two approaches on the table. Let's start the discussion." Ownership is far less important than the fact that the group has the advantage of two ideas, both of which everyone should want to consider and evaluate.

Openness

Effective climates are marked by openness—the perceived freedom to express and explore ideas without fear of ridicule, intimidation, or attack. Like cooperativeness, openness is created and sustained through members' communicative choices throughout discussion. To encourage an open climate, members should strive for active, balanced participation by all (Harper & Askling, 1980). You want to demonstrate that you trust other members and that you are trustworthy. Be careful not to make derogatory evaluations. Nobody should be penalized for an honest effort. After a few harsh criticisms are voiced, communication may stop: Who wants to jump into piranha-infested waters? Even if you think a comment is foolish, diplomacy is in order. How you respond has an impact beyond a specific exchange—it influences the overall group climate by indicating to all members how ideas may be treated.

> Have you been in a situation where a group member did not take your ideas seriously? What did they say? What did you do? How did you feel?

The manner in which you advance your ideas can foster or discourage openness. We encourage you to offer ideas in a way that suggests you are open to other ideas or to criticisms and modifications. We are not advising you to be timid, but we are cautioning against dogmatism and zealotry. Phrases such as "Perhaps we could consider another way of going about this," or "I have a suggestion all of us might be able to refine and build on" keep the channels for discussion open and invite teamwork.

Don't forget—you need to be open-minded in order to keep an open climate. If you push for your own ideas, become overly-sensitive if someone wants to modify something you proposed, or operate with a hidden agenda, then you are contributing to a non-cooperative climate. The choice is yours.

Rhetorical Sensitivity

As discussed in chapter 4, rhetorical sensitivity is an attitude that honors the person speaking, the people listening, and the integrity of communication itself. Rhetorically-sensitive communication aims for a balanced recognition of speakers' and listeners' rights and responsibilities. While certain kinds of hateful speech may be protected by your right to free speech, a rhetorically-sensitive speaker would never say anything that intentionally offends or hurts another group member. Effective, sensitive listening and speaking are two halves of a whole, and they are equally important in creating an ideal climate for discussion and constructive conflict management. As an effective group member, you should think carefully, choose words carefully, and respect the audience.

CONFLICT RESOLUTION STYLES

No matter how carefully you work toward a constructive communication climate, at one point or another you are bound to run into disruptive conflict. You can resolve conflict more quickly and effectively if you learn to recognize frequently used styles of responding to conflict. Conflict styles are patterned responses—the tactics an individual most frequently uses when in a conflict situation (Wilmot & Hocker, 2007). Most of us use one or two styles most often and rarely use the rest. However, to be an effective group member, you should analyze each situation and use the style that fits the situation. The following styles are based on work by Ralph Kilmann and Kenneth Thomas (1977), and we have added a few additional styles as well.

Avoidance is a common response to conflict. The participant walks away or withdraws or changes the topic to avoid conflict. Take Shavonne, for example. When group members disagree with one another, Shavonne becomes uncomfortable. She will joke around with the members to distract them from the disagreement. If that doesn't work, she will often get up and leave for a while. While avoidance is the appropriate way to react when there is any fear of physical or verbal abuse, it can lead to some problems in standard group discussion. When Shavonne jokes around, other members may think that she is not taking the discussion seriously, which leads to incorrect assumptions about her dedication to the group. If she leaves, she is no longer available to help with the problem solving. The group misses her valuable contributions. On the other hand, if she feels that she will say something negative that will harm interpersonal relationships in the group, then it might be best for her to leave until she cools down. There are some subsets of avoidance as well. **Withdrawing** happens when someone doesn't care to engage in the conflict. This can happen for two reasons: (1) John has no opinion on the topic or no needs that must be met. In this case, he truly doesn't care about the issue. (2) Sandra is truly afraid of conflict. Because she grew up in an abusive family, emotionally she can't handle it when people start to raise their voices or argue back and forth even in good spirit. Another subset of avoidance is *delaying*. Delaying happens when someone is too upset to continue with the conflict at that moment. LaQuicha knows she is about to say something that she'll regret, so she tells her group she can't talk about it right now, but she will come prepared to discuss it at the next meeting or after a 10-minute break.

Accommodation is a style marked by always giving in to the other members, even at the expense of a member's own desires. As an example, Javier is from Spain. Because of his cultural differences, he can often see things from a different perspective. However, he often feels out of place. Unfortunately, he is an accommodator—because he sees himself as an outsider, he does not want to rock the boat. He wants to get along with everyone in the group, so he will give in to the ideas of the group rather than risk being perceived as different. While the group may remain friendly, they will miss the contributions his insightful perspectives could make toward a better solution. In instances where Javier doesn't care about a particular decision being made by the group (i.e. what to order for a snack), accommodation is a good choice. Do make sure that if you give into the group, you don't hold it over their heads at a later time. No one enjoys a member who plays the martyr.

Competition is a style where the participant views the conflict as a contest and will do everything possible to win. Ryan uses this style. Every time there is a conflict, he will assert his point until everyone else gets fed up and gives in. It doesn't matter to Ryan whether he is right or wrong: he simply has to "win." The competitive style disrupts group discussion where collective goals are important. This style might be appropriate if there is a crisis decision that must be made immediately. In that case, the leader may need to dictate a resolution. You might also use the competitive style if you care deeply about an idea or are positive you are right. However, if you are in basic group discussion, relying heavily on this style can turn into **bullying**, particularly with a style like Ryan's. If you are trying to hammer things out in the spirit of inquiry, know when to stop.

Compromise is a style where one participant will give in a little as long as another participant does the same. Laura, for example, is a good compromiser. She can usually see the "middle mark" between two positions. Compromise can sometimes be useful in group discussion if all of the avenues of information have been explored. There will be times when the group cannot come to a conclusion or decision. In this case it makes sense for members to engage in give and take.

Collaboration involves careful review of the information with the other group members. Interpretations and ideas are discussed until members reach an agreement. Collaboration is the most useful style to use in group problem-solving discussions. It does take a tremendous amount of time in some instances, however. Groups need to be committed to the discussion process and to work hard to keep the climate right for this type of conflict resolution. If your group is rushed or apathetic, collaboration probably will not occur. You need to ensure that everyone has the right to speak his or her mind and is ready to analyze issues critically. An atmosphere that allows for collaboration will help make the problem-solving process even more effective.

How can you use this information? Think carefully about which style you tend to use most often. Your instructor may help you fill out an inventory to clarify your preferred style. Do you adapt your style? Or do you use the same one all of the time?

Think carefully about your own style and discuss the styles used by others. People with different backgrounds tend to rely on different styles. For instance, if Tom grew up in an authoritative household where his step-dad always laid down the law and no one questioned it, he is possibly going to be an accommodator or an avoider—he really had no other choice growing up. On the other hand, Akiem grew up in a household where spirited discussion was the norm. His mom encouraged healthy discussion and argument to encourage his critical thinking skills. Akiem is most likely going to be a competitor and collaborator. Unfortunately, if you put these two people together without an understanding of styles and one another, Akiem will probably think that Tom has no backbone, and Tom will be put off by Akiem's assertive style. Sometimes simply talking about how individuals communicate can be helpful. Akiem might say, "Hey Tom, I notice you seem to shut down when I try to argue points. I want you to know I'm not attacking you—I just enjoy the activity of discussing ideas."

GROUPTHINK

So what happens when there is no conflict in the group? When all members enthusiastically accept and agree with each other's ideas, the group could be a victim of "groupthink." Irving Janis (1972), a noted sociologist, defined groupthink as the phenomenon wherein individual members suppress their personal ideas and their attitudes in order to reach agreement and to preserve friendly, cohesive relations in a group.

Groupthink has two important characteristics. First, group members unconsciously suppress ideas and critical attitudes. Nobody comes right out and says, "Let's have no disagreements." Instead, members fail to recognize issues that need to be explored, questions that ought to be raised, or positions that should be challenged. They unconsciously become less critical of each other's ideas.

Second, groupthink cannot be explained in terms of individual psychology. It is a group phenomenon that occurs because of the dynamics that happen during group interaction. Members' critical faculties are paralyzed because an overall norm, which emphasizes agreement, overtakes the group. They become unable to see points where disagreement would be appropriate. As you might predict, the result tends to be sloppy decision making.

Please realize we are not saying conformity is necessarily bad. Sometimes people change their positions because they have been persuaded by legitimate means (reasons, evidence). This is called **reasoned consent**, and it is valuable in group discussion. However, when people give up ideas just to avoid rocking the boat or when they cease to think critically, the result is injury to the entire group and its goals.

Since groupthink undermines problem solving and since it is very difficult to detect once it has taken hold, it is important for all discussants to recognize its early symptoms.

Symptoms of Groupthink

Every group has norms about how agreement is reached. But there are four symptoms of groupthink with which your group should be familiar.

- Accepting agreement without discussion or examination
- Believing the group is invulnerable
- Rationalizing away undesirable information
- Developing and promoting negative stereotypes of outsiders.

When a group seems to *value agreement above all* and is willing to accept it on any terms, it is a sign of groupthink. When an idea is first voiced in your group, do other members nod assent or offer verbal reinforcement? If so, you may be experiencing groupthink. In this situation, members do not ask questions or challenge evidence, nor do they argue, typically because members have unconsciously turned off their critical thinking capacities in the interest of achieving harmony and saving time. Members retain a sense of security, because each person feels that "if we agree, the idea must be right."

In a situation of uniform consensus, "we" feelings overpower respect for the rights of individuals. Anyone who disagrees is regarded as an opponent of the group, a barrier to progress, an undesirable member. Usually the group just ignores them until they leave of their own accord. If "undesirables" keep on disagreeing, they are nudged out of the group. If they resist, they are thrown out.

A second major symptom of groupthink is members' belief that their group is *invulnerable*. This illusion of invulnerability is cherished because members can feel secure when they can convince themselves their group can do no wrong. Typically, members think their group has unlimited power and is incapable of error. As you might predict, this attitude can lead to rash decision making and inadequate analysis of ideas. If your group no longer has any healthy skepticism, if members do not check for contradictory ideas, and if they refuse to consider the possibilities of problems inherent in plans, the group is bound to make mistakes. Most frightening of all is the probability that no one will notice the mistakes because members have an overriding interest in maintaining consensus, no matter how uninformed it may be.

Rationalization is a third symptom of groupthink. It is the process that minimizes evidence that threatens the group's plans. Members rationalize away any contradictory information in order to sustain the group's prized sense of unanimity and rightness. This allows members to label contrary evidence as false, to discount warnings as unfounded, to wave off all disagreement as contentiousness, and to impugn the motives of those who object.

A fourth symptom of groupthink is developing and promoting *negative stereotypes* of outsiders. Anyone not in the group may be branded as

> Have you ever found yourself finishing a group project and asking some-one to review your work? What happens when that person makes sugges-tions? Do you immediately rationalize that they don't know what they are talking about? Maybe they didn't really understand the assignment? Think carefully when you start to rationalize.

"the enemy" or as inferior to the select few who hold membership. Members enmeshed in groupthink strengthen themselves by defining outsiders as competitors. Members pull even more tightly together to combat the enemy, often an effective strategy in team sports. In other cases, members stereotype anyone outside the group as incompetent or ineffective. While this may boost morale, the danger for group discussion members is that they eliminate sources that could offer interesting perspectives on the problem to be solved. Isolated thinking usually yields very limited solutions at best.

No group is immune to groupthink, so it is important that members be able to recognize early warning signs of the phenomenon. Anytime you find yourself agreeing with collective positions too quickly, suspect groupthink. Anytime you find yourself discounting opinions of outsiders that differ from those of the group, be wary. Anytime you sense overconfidence about group powers, back up and reconsider your position.

> **Research Check**
>
> Several researchers found that members who had limited information were more likely to conform to pressure from other group members than were members who had "full information conditions." "In the current study, we examined the symptoms of groupthink. Unlike traditional approaches to groupthink (e.g., Janis, 1972), we argued that these symptoms reflect two different processes that may occur in decision-making groups: reinforcement and compliance" (Henningsen, Henningsen, Eden, & Cruz, 2006, pp. 59–60).

Correctives to Groupthink

Once groupthink is established and becomes the norm, there is usually little that can be done. We will offer three suggestions to help you build a group climate that does not allow the development of groupthink. These suggestions will help you respond if you detect early symptoms of groupthink.

Minimize the status differences among members. High-status members have the potential to influence other members, so all group members should work toward establishing a tone that welcomes probing questions. One factor that helps achieve this is having higher-status individuals speak after other ideas are presented. High-status individuals should monitor their behaviors. If the leader, for instance, notices that others are accepting his/her ideas uncritically, he/she should bring that to the attention of the group and reserve comments or suggestions until others have contributed.

Appoint a devil's advocate if members are not questioning ideas. If someone has the role to question all ideas and to represent minority points of view, then the group can help to avoid groupthink. A member can be a devil's advocate without being overbearing. In fact, if done well, devil's advocacy can become contagious. You might also consider inviting an outsider to sit in to play devil's advocate during some of your sessions.

Develop a norm that legitimizes disagreement in discussion. It is important to demonstrate that questioning and challenging are methods for furthering group goals, not individual egos; this should be done from the onset. All members can advance ideas tentatively ("What do you think about X" rather than "I think we should . . .") to promote questioning and criticism. The time that you put into fostering a climate where members feel free to critically analyze ideas will contribute to effective decision making.

Research Check

Annette Flippen (1999) examined how the motivation of members, particularly the leader, might lead to groupthink and suggested that traditional correctives may not be appropriate. Traditional correctives assume "that the group and its leader are indeed motivated to find the best solution to the problem and are just having trouble doing so. . . . Do they [the leader] act in this manner because they believe that this is the best way of leading the group or are they trying to promote their own agenda? If they do have the best interests of the group in mind, then training them not to promote their own ideas too early may indeed be effective, but if their main goal is the acceptance of their ideas and the increase of their power then all the training the world may not change their behavior. In this situation, it would perhaps be better to focus on making them accountable both for the end product of the group and for the amount of participation on the part of the group members. . . . Similarly, training group members how to speak up will not be effective if they are self-regulating in terms of whether they have the approval of the leader or other members, rather than in terms of whether the group has arrived at a quality solution. In this case, they are not speaking up because they do not wish to, not because they do not know how to" (pp. 158–159).

ADDITIONAL TROUBLESHOOTING

We've described ideals for group climate, so you should have a good idea of what kind of tone you want. To establish and sustain an effective climate, you will need to monitor constantly for signs of any problems.

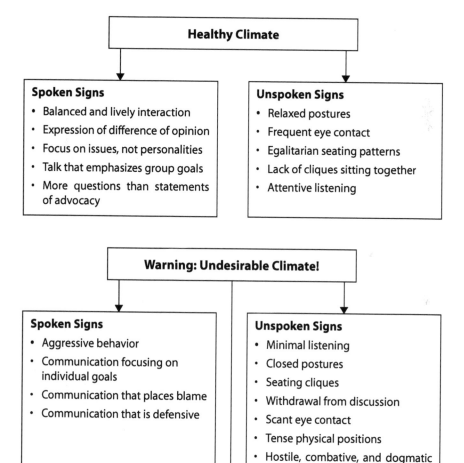

Healthy Climate

Spoken Signs
- Balanced and lively interaction
- Expression of difference of opinion
- Focus on issues, not personalities
- Talk that emphasizes group goals
- More questions than statements of advocacy

Unspoken Signs
- Relaxed postures
- Frequent eye contact
- Egalitarian seating patterns
- Lack of cliques sitting together
- Attentive listening

Warning: Undesirable Climate!

Spoken Signs
- Aggressive behavior
- Communication focusing on individual goals
- Communication that places blame
- Communication that is defensive

Unspoken Signs
- Minimal listening
- Closed postures
- Seating cliques
- Withdrawal from discussion
- Scant eye contact
- Tense physical positions
- Hostile, combative, and dogmatic tone

Other Signs
- Either excessive cohesion or lack of cohesion
- Lack of critical, reflective thought
- Presence of groupthink
- Lack of trust among members
- Little effort to work cooperatively

If you spot any of these warning signs, you should attempt to correct the climate before a negative tone is established. One way to correct it is by modeling appropriate communicative choices. If you refuse to join in with someone who is attacking personalities and instead guide the discussion back to the issue, you are making a good communication choice. Others will pick up on your style and respond similarly. And if they don't, then you can suggest more directly, "Sam, let's keep our comments focused on the issue."

It may also be appropriate to call an intermission in task work and, as a group, analyze the climate. There's no need for heavy disclosure or amateur psychoanalysis of members' motives for behavior. It is possible, however, to talk in a civilized way about what is going on in the group and to collectively generate some ways of correcting shared problems. The group may be able to devise some useful rules to guide deliberations.

One group we observed, for instance, analyzed the climate and recognized competitiveness creeping into their interaction. To remedy the problem, they developed this list of communication rules:

1. Interruptions are not allowed. The person speaking has the floor until he or she finishes.

2. The first response to an idea may *not* be negative. If we need to criticize an idea, that comes after responses that recognize the contribution and its meritorious aspects.

3. We will not have sideline conversations between members while someone is talking.

4. When two or more members seem locked in disagreement, they will be asked to meet together to work out a mutually acceptable position.

The group found these rules useful in helping break some undesirable habits that were beginning to interfere with effective problem solving. After several meetings where the rules were rigidly enforced, members found they no longer needed to police their communication. They had developed different and more productive communication norms and consequently had promoted a much healthier climate in which to work.

✗ 7 ✗

Standard Agenda Step One
Understanding the Charge

The primary goal of the first step of the standard agenda is to figure out what your group is supposed to do. It is imperative that your group completely understands and agrees on what it is supposed to accomplish so that everyone works toward a common goal. Once your group understands the task, it can begin to examine the options for accomplishing that task.

✗ Goals of Step One ✗

Eager to get to the issues and tasks that lie ahead, groups often overlook the initial steps of discussion. Group leaders and chairs have been known to say, "I think you all know why we're here, so I won't waste time going into that." Unfortunately, some people may be unclear about why they are there. Since employees often advance based on their group performance, they think that if they ask for direction they will appear to be incompetent. As a result, they may assume that everyone else understands what is going on, and they may refrain from asking questions. In step one, the group should:

- Understand the charge.
- Ascertain their authority.
- Assess their resources.
- Determine when they will be done.
- Assess the legitimacy of a topic.

UNDERSTANDING THE CHARGE

The *charge* is the task that has been assigned to a group by its governing body: a supervisor, a teacher, a president of an organization, etc. The best way to begin the problem-solving process is to make sure that everyone in the group understands the charge. Are you supposed to solve a problem? Write a report? Make a recommendation? Suggest solutions so someone else can solve the problem? It is important that everyone in the group is clear as to what the group is supposed to do so there is unity in the process. If the necessary amount of time is not spent establishing a clear understanding of the charge, each member may operate according to his or her own ideas. Tremendous problems may arise without a clear understanding of the task.

So what happens if a group is unclear about its task? Task forces in organizations, for example, spend hours of work and personal time solving problems that impact many people. Without a clear purpose, uninformed members sometimes unknowingly go beyond their authority, do sloppy work, solve problems that do not exist, or fail to solve the assigned problem. At a minimum, they waste company money; in extreme cases, they can ruin a company's image. As an example, one author of this book served on a committee that recommended faculty members for promotions. The committee chair never clarified the charge. After hours of discussing the materials each applicant provided, it became evident that the members were judging the faculty in different ways. Some only considered the information the faculty member provided. Others, who knew the faculty member, wanted to consider information that the applicant had failed to provide. Once the group understood the charge—to judge only the information provided—the group reached a decision more quickly and with less conflict.

Key Questions for Understanding the Assignment or Charge

Always make sure to clarify the charge (in writing if possible). Be sure to obtain clear answers to the following questions:

- What output is desired? (Are you writing a formal document? Presenting the outcome to an audience?)
- Do you choose your own problem? (Be sure you understand your limitations.)
- What are your instructions? (Make sure everyone understands them.)
- How will you be evaluated? (Does your boss judge the output? In a class, does everyone get the same grade? What are the policies for reporting slackers?)

ASCERTAINING YOUR AUTHORITY

Determining the authority of the group is directly related to analyzing the group's charge. There is no sense in spending months developing a wonderful strategic plan to eliminate college classes on all Fridays if the group has no power to implement that plan.

Often, the classroom group has little power; no one has to cooperate with it. The group has no budget, and anything that gets done has to be done by the people in the group. They have responsibility, but no authority. However, many groups without power have been able to achieve significant gains. Neighborhood improvement groups, social action groups, disgruntled employee groups, and protest groups have all been known to start with no authority, no resources, and little power, yet they sometimes change the entire community or an organization with their efforts.

Once your group is aware of its authority, you need to make sure you don't overstep it. Sometimes groups make recommendations that make their superiors look bad, overstep boundaries, or are in bad taste. For example, imagine your group is charged with making a proposal for boosting employee morale. If you focus on planning a special event and your boss is the chair of the special events committee, you have just overstepped your boundaries and possibly made your boss look bad for not coming up with the idea him/herself. By understanding the chain of command and the group's position, you can make recommendations that will be better received by superiors and, thus, more likely to be implemented.

Whether your group has total authority or none, the members must immediately understand what they are up against. By doing so, they will not waste their time or make procedural mistakes.

ASSESS YOUR RESOURCES

Each group needs to assess what resources are available. Do you have a budget? Are you willing to contribute personal money? Is grant money available? Have you explored all avenues of funding? In addition to money, do you have meeting spaces and supplies? Equipment? On a member level, what skills does each member bring to the group? What skills do you need that no one has? Where can you find someone with these skills? Are there other resources you need to assess?

We know of numerous organizations that pay a lot of money to bring in speakers and experts when they have those resources within their own company. Outside experts are not always necessary if an organization realizes the strengths of its own employees. We have also seen student groups who did not realize their members had no editing skills. Imagine how this oversight could affect a written report. Both examples are costly errors of resource assessment.

KNOWING WHEN YOU ARE DONE

Another important matter to understand is when and how the group will know that the problem has been solved and their task is finished. With some groups' charges, this is easy. If you are reviewing candidates for a position, your work is over when you hand in a list of recommendations. Other groups are given a specific deadline. In some groups, however, knowing when you are done is much more difficult. In such cases, the group should anticipate possible problems and set goals for assessing when they are finished.

For example, a group of concerned citizens trying to reduce accidents on a busy highway could set "elimination of accidents" as its end point or solution. That solution might take forever to reach. This group needs to set several intermediate solutions: (1) pressuring the city council for a traffic census, (2) asking the state highway commission for a traffic light, (3) getting it installed, and (4) petitioning the police for extra patrols at peak traffic hours. They might consider their work to be finished when they have thoroughly analyzed the problem, written a comprehensive report and implemented their best solution. Most groups present their solutions in oral or written reports as the final indicator that the project is complete.

LEGITIMACY OF TOPICS

Some additional considerations apply to groups who are doing class assignments. If your group is allowed to choose its own topic, you need to choose carefully. Remember that members will be more motivated to work on assignments they like. The topic must also be "do-able." "How can we eliminate racial prejudice?" or "What should be U.S. policy on terrorism?" are complex problems with complex solutions. Rather than waste time on questions that the group cannot answer, spend some time focusing on a question that is at the group's level and one in which a solution may be implemented.

A reasonable question might be, "What is the most important thing that students on this campus could do to combat racial prejudice?" By focusing the question on racism "at the university" and by focusing on one "doable" action, the time spent on the research project will not be wasted. The solutions could be sent to a campus administrator for possible implementation.

℀ Outcomes of Step One ℀

Preliminary discussions about your assignment should focus on what your group needs to know about (1) the solution, and (2) the rights, privileges, duties, and obligations of the group. With these items clear, the group is on its way to achieving the desired end. At the end of this phase of discussion, the members should have a written record of their understanding of the charge.

WRITTEN RECORD OF THE GROUP'S UNDERSTANDING

One member needs to be designated as the record keeper. Some groups, especially those functioning within organizational settings, may have the services of an administrative assistant, who will prepare and distribute minutes of meetings. Taking notes may be time consuming, but the effort is worthwhile and necessary. As the project develops, someone may question a decision or an idea. It is much more reliable to refer to a written record than to try to remember what was said.

> How often have you been in a group where no record is kept of its decisions? Have you heard members say, "Now what was it we decided at the last meeting?" Careful record keeping can eliminate wasted hours and flaring tempers.

According to Alice Sturgis (2001), minutes should contain the following:
- Date, hour, and place of the meeting
- Time the meeting was called to order
- All motions with the name of the proposer and the outcome of the vote
- Summary of each report with the name of the person presenting it
- A record of all decisions made by the body (p. 200-201)

Also according to Sturgis, minutes should not contain:
- Personal opinions, interpretations or comments by the secretary
- Descriptive or judgmental phrases (p. 201).

Minutes need to be signed by the recorder and distributed as soon as possible after meetings. Members should review the minutes before the next scheduled meeting.

While there are hundreds of formats, one of the formats that we use personally is in the form of a table.

Department of Communication & Theatre Minutes		
DATE: 8/26/99	TIME: 12:30–2:00 PM	PLACE: SH 416
PRESENT: List by last name or first name depending on formality		
Topic	**Points of Discussion**	**Decision or Action**
Introductions	New faculty introduced.	
JN 100	Journalism 100 course added to schedule. Course will meet T–Th 2:00–3:15, AH G22.	Faculty should announce to students.
Auditions for fall productions	Auditions will be next week for fall productions.	Faculty should encourage students to try out.
Communication day	Date set for April 14.	Faculty should remind students of date.
New course proposal for Gender Comm.	Smith: Gender already covered in interpersonal. Wood: Gender is a recognized concentration area of its own. Class is offered at other schools like ours. Motion by Young.	Motion carried. 9 in favor, 1 opposed. Chair will send proposal to Academic Affairs Committee.
Adjourned at 1:15		
Submitted by: Xernalia Smith		

QUESTIONS ABOUT THE CHARGE

For some groups, especially those established from higher in the chain of command, the precise charge may be put in writing. This can serve as a loose contract between the group and the issuing authority. However, even in writing, charges can sometimes be unclear.

The group should list any and every question that they have about the charge, even if some members feel they understand a particular question raised. The group should (1) review the limits of authority so they can determine the most appropriate communication style and (2) examine the best way to approach the person who issued the charge. Should the leader be the contact person? Should an official communicator be designated? In industry, who is best suited to ask questions of the boss? the VP? the CEO? How will the group be perceived? As inquisitive and thorough? Or as a nuisance?

When you are finished with this phase of step one, you should have a written record of all points of discussion and understanding thus far.

ℑ Member Tasks in Step One ℐ

In the first six chapters of this book, we presented basic guidelines for discussion. Understanding these guidelines and selecting behaviors that support and demonstrate them are important individual responsibilities throughout all stages of group discussion. This is especially true for step one. Enthusiastic, informed participation by all members helps establish a cooperative tone and style for future deliberations. This sets the stage for effective interactions and relationships that contribute to the thoroughness, efficiency, and ultimate productivity of your group.

BECOMING FAMILIAR WITH COLLEAGUES

Before you begin anything, it is important to get to know the people with whom you are working. There are a few things that you will want to know about others in your group.

- Why is each person in the group?
- What do they like or dislike about working in groups?
- What do they want to get out of the group experience?
- What interpersonal needs does each person have?
- What skills does each person have that will contribute to the project?
- What are the expectations for behavior in the group?
- Do you want a team contract?

Research Check

You should note that this list would contain different items if you are in a non-American culture. For example, the fact that family is the first priority for people in Mexican culture "is communicated through a wide range of behaviors including asking questions about colleagues' families, discussing personal matters before business (e.g. at the beginning of meeting), taking action to promote employees' personal well-being, including families in organizational activities, taking time off work to assist family members in need, and establishing, developing, and maintaining long-term interconnected networks of personal relationships" (Lindsley & Braithwaite, 2006, p. 283).

There are different reasons why people may be in a group. They may have been assigned to the group, or they may have volunteered. If they are assigned, are they pleased with the assignment or are they angry about it? If everyone there is happy and committed, you may not have to do a lot to achieve cohesion. If they are angry about the assignment, however, the group leader may want to explore some interpersonal exercises to allow the team members to get to know one another and to build some bonds.

You might also address what members like and dislike about working in groups. Many people do not like to rely on other people. Some do not like the scheduling conflicts or getting to know new people. If a group takes the time to listen to the concerns that members have, they can talk about ways to ensure that those concerns will not be a problem in their particular group. It can also be motivational to hear what members like about working in groups. Being reminded that sharing a workload makes the job easier or that groups often solve problems better than individuals working alone can be a motivational springboard for your project.

It is also important to talk about what each member wants to get out of the group experience. Often, a member's unhappiness in a group is a direct result of unclear expectations. Some members may expect to work out-of-class, while others are unwilling to do so; some may want to earn an "A," while others are satisfied with a "C." In the corporate world, some members may want to write the best report the boss has ever seen while others realize the boss never reads the reports; therefore, they just want to do enough to get by. These conflicts in expectations and motivations can create a number of problems if they are not revealed early. If the group knows about the differences at the beginning, then they can distribute the workload in a more effective manner and create a climate that will benefit everyone.

Interpersonal preferences are another area that the group can discuss. What motivates each member interpersonally? What type of person is each member? Some people are task oriented while others are socially oriented. Some people like to work on their own while others like companionship. Some people like lots of positive reinforcement while others are self-sufficient. Some people have an interpersonal pet peeve such as becoming annoyed if people do not look at them when they are talking. The more you know about each group member on an interpersonal level, the easier it will be to work with them. While it may seem strange at first to talk about your interpersonal preferences, taking 10 minutes to share them can save many hard feelings and awkward situations down the road.

In addition to knowing each member's expectations and interpersonal preferences, it is also a good idea to take an inventory of member skills and work preferences. To have the best outcome, members need to be assigned to tasks they enjoy and at which they can excel. Who likes to collaborate? Who likes to work alone? If a person prefers solo work, they might be the best researcher. Who has technical skills or knowledge that the group might need? Who is best suited to keeping records and handling arrangements for meetings? Highly detail-oriented members make the best record keepers and proofreaders. By spending a few minutes discussing these questions, your group can share feelings and determine ways to circumvent misunderstandings that distract from understanding and completing the charge.

Group members will also want to share their expectations for behavior in the group. Whether you are doing a classroom project or working on a corporate committee, members need to be in agreement about absences, lateness, preparedness, and rules of order. What constitutes an excused absence? How late may members arrive? Do they need an excuse? Will you discuss informally or will you use Robert's Rules of Order? Talking about these issues should enable you to determine whether or not you'd like to design a team contract.

A team contract can be useful for accountability, particularly in student groups. The contract outlines the working expectations for each group member. It may also detail the penalties for not meeting the agreed upon expectations. If you have a team contract and a member does not meet the expectations, it makes it much easier to punish the member since he/she agreed upon the expectations, and the group has it in writing.

One example of team contract has six sections

1. A team goal.

2. A list of what each member will do.

3. A list of what each member will not do.

4. A list of penalty points for each of the items in numbers 2 and 3: For example, "For each missed meeting, a member will lose 5 points for an excused absence (defined as . . .) and 10 points for an unexcused absence (defined as . . .). Think ahead for potential problems.

Research Check

If you have the option to evaluate one another, you may want to determine whether you will do this once at the end of the project or multiple times throughout the project. Simon Tagger and Travor Brown (2006) found that initial peer ratings influenced future peer ratings on tasks in a classroom setting. "Leniency is more common when a person receives positive peer feedback, severity is more common when a person receives negative peer feedback. . . . Our results suggest the need for managers to obtain feedback from multiple sources (e.g., clients, managers, subordinates, self) in addition to peers. Managers should ensure that all raters, including peers, are trained in how to use the appraisal instrument and how to minimize potential rating errors" (pp. 100, 102).

5. A list of the roles of team members (include the leader, recorder, and others).

6. A list of strengths of each participating member.

If you have no method of member assessment, then points are irrelevant. But you may still do well to use the expectation section as a motivational tool and to make sure that everyone is on the same page.

EXERCISING YOUR OPTIONS

Always remember that you have some control over how the group is managed. You can choose to ask questions about the nature of the task. If the leader begins with "we all know why we are here" and you have doubts about that assessment, ask questions. Encourage group members to focus on the questions we have included in this chapter.

Asserting Your Position in the Group

It is best to be honest and open with group members before the group begins working on the task. If you have family or work obligations that will preclude you from participating to the fullest extent, reveal those obligations immediately so that you can negotiate solutions before tensions run high. If you are less than motivated about the project, be honest, but also be prepared for the possible consequences of that revelation. While other members may appreciate your honesty, some may be less than happy about your attitude. Be very clear about what you expect from others and what you are willing to give to the group. If this is clarified accurately at the beginning, the group tends to function much more effectively. Again, many problems in a group are a direct result of conflicting and unclear expectations. If your group goes through the steps listed above about getting to know one another, it is your ethical responsibility to be truthful when answering those questions.

> Tim will be satisfied with a "C" in the class. He is unwilling to work on the project beyond a minimal contribution. You are an "A" student and very much want to keep your 4.0 GPA. What kind of negotiation might you make with Tim?

Being Flexible

There are multiple demands on one's time in today's world. While each member will have a tightly packed personal schedule, each must also remain somewhat flexible to the group. In order to function effectively as a group, you will need to have meetings. It is rare to find a meeting time that is considered ideal for all members. You have probably worked with someone who claims, "I can only meet on Wednesdays from 9–9:30. Every other time during the week, I have other obligations." This person really could meet at 3:00 PM on Fridays or at 7:00 AM but wants to do something else at those times. This person is inflexible.

Take a look at schedules, negotiate, and come up with what is best for everyone. If there is truly no good time, then consider options: (1) this week inconvenience one member, then the next week inconvenience a different member, and/or (2) the group can meet in subgroups and then a representative from each can get together. There are always options; sometimes finding one involves a good deal of give and take.

Your group also needs to be realistic when determining how long a meeting will last. A meeting scheduled for 30 minutes can last two hours because of lack of preparation or unexpected problems. Effective groups will have a realistic plan and will be able to handle unexpected delays. They will also plan a start time and an end time to show respect for members' busy schedules. Be sure to adhere to the time schedule for every meeting.

To be a responsible member of a group, you must invest your time and be flexible when unexpected events upset the schedule. If you are a volunteer member and anticipate that work or family demands will conflict with the group's needs, you should probably terminate your membership at the outset. It is frustrating for more committed members to have to replace someone in the group during a crucial time or to have to take up the slack created by less committed members.

Maintaining Orderly Procedure and Task Focus

Although this usually falls under the leader's obligations, members also can help to maintain order. While a brief social element is necessary at the beginning of meetings, the group must stay focused in order to finish the task. For example, if Mark is distracted by the conversation between two members, he hurts the group if he doesn't politely point it out.

Avoiding Premature Decisions

In some cases, a group member or members try to solve the problem too quickly. The leader and members should be careful to avoid this problem. If members are too anxious to get the task completed, they may force a vote on an issue. If members select a solution early, they preclude considering relevant information that has yet to be collected. That missing information could stimulate ideas that may offer better alternatives. Stay alert to warning signs about conclusions being drawn too early. Solid conclusions often require patience.

Establishing Your Image

Your image with group members is often shaped during initial sessions. During step one, you should concentrate on making a variety of contributions: offer information, guide discussions, and critically analyze other ideas so members know you are an interested participant in all group undertakings. A motivated person is consistent in their behavior. If you are interested in performing a specialized service to the group, such as leading or recording, now is also the time to reveal those preferences.

⚂ Leader Obligations in Step One ⚄

If a leader was not designated in the assignment, the group must decide who will perform this function. While a leaderless discussion is possible, it is important to know where final decision-making responsibility lies. Someone must be in charge of keeping records, acting as liaison with the authorities, and delegating responsibilities. It is imperative to agree on the who and how of leadership in step one of the discussion.

> Denzel and Tamara both want to be the leader for the group project. They have both specifically stated that it is important for them to have this position, and they do not like working in groups where they cannot be leader. How should the group handle this?

CHOOSING A LEADERSHIP STYLE

It is important to find out what type of leadership the group desires. Groups whose members have a limited interest in the project and work best by following orders would do best with an autocratic leader. Other groups need a leader who integrates ideas and acts as a facilitator; a more democratic approach would fit such groups. No matter what kind of leader is appropriate, it is extremely important that leadership style is a group decision. Members may rebel if they are led in a way that is not consistent with their expectations. A leader can best motivate others when they know an individual's expectations.

PREPARING FOR THE LEADERSHIP ROLE

A person who agrees to be the leader has the added responsibilities of agenda planning, moderating discussion, and acting as liaison with the governing authority. Leaders need to be prepared to share what the governing body tells them so that the group feels included as well. If the leader attends meetings unprepared, there is little hope that the group will be effective. They also need to be prepared to deal with interpersonal conflicts and issues in a fair and consistent manner.

SETTING A LEADERSHIP TONE

The tone of leadership style tends to be set at early meetings. By encouraging members to talk and by giving their questions careful attention, the leader encourages participation. If questions cannot be answered immediately, the leader should clearly specify who is responsible for providing the answers in time for the next meeting. A leader should not be afraid to divide the tasks among the members. By passing questions to others, leaders indicate that they welcome cooperation in leadership, thus encouraging other members to engage in leadership acts. The spirit of goodwill necessary to move the group ahead requires sharing the work. Goodwill does not necessarily mean that members socialize and be good friends; rather, it means that all should be knowledgeable, willing, and responsive to everyone's efforts.

TAKING LEADERSHIP RESPONSIBILITY

Leaders also have negative responsibilities at times. If a member is not doing his or her part of the workload, the leader is usually the first person to address the problem. This can be an uncomfortable position, both in the classroom and in industry. If there is a firing policy for the group, the leader must know that policy and abide by it. He/she must be willing to have difficult meetings. Of course, if the expectations of group members were clear from the beginning, then handling a member who is not doing his/her share becomes much easier. However, even when justified, many people find it difficult to comment on a peer's performance. Think carefully about the responsibility of leaders to handle negative situations. If you don't want to play such a role, do not volunteer for the position.

You are the leader of your group. One of the members, Stephanie, has not attended three of the last four meetings. At the one meeting she did attend, she worked on homework for another class while the other group members discussed the project. She has handed in her research to the group, but it is so poorly done that someone will have to redo the work. You have asked to see Stephanie after the next meeting. What will you say to her?

WRAPPING IT UP

The leader's final obligation in the first stage is to make certain that all agreements are recorded and that there is a plan for the remainder of the meetings. Once again, the pattern of keeping careful records that are made available to all should be set at the first meeting.

AN UNSPOKEN CONTRACT FOR SERIOUS GROUP PROBLEM SOLVING

To conclude this chapter, we want to review what we have said about group discussion in general. This review takes the form of a statement of the obligations assumed by each individual group member, an unspoken contract. The idea for the unspoken contract that appears below was inspired by Carroll C. Arnold's (1974) "Unspoken Contract for Serious Oral Communication." You may also want to consider writing a real contract for the group members.

> I am not here to waste my time, to make idle chatter, or to solve my personal and emotional problems. I am not here to make friends or do combat with enemies. I am here for a purpose, and I suspect that the others here have a purpose as well. I do not expect them to agree with me or to support me in all things I do, but I expect them, like me, to be reasonably dedicated to the accomplishment of the group task that brought us here in the first place.
>
> I know I cannot handle this problem alone. If I could have I would have, because I know that working with a group takes time and effort, and like all other human beings, I would prefer to do the best job I can in the easiest possible way. We all have strengths and weaknesses; together we can pool our strengths and overcome our weaknesses.
>
> I have the obligation to speak up, to make my point of view known. If I just sit here, I will waste my time and the time of others. I must present my ideas clearly so that others can understand them well enough to criticize them sensibly, and I must listen to the ideas of others in a critical but not hostile way. It is my job to analyze what is said and to report the results of my analysis.
>
> I understand that group problem solving is not a haphazard enterprise. I am prepared to curb my enthusiasm and impatience and to follow the steps that will raise our chances of reaching a logical, effective, and well-reasoned solution.
>
> I have the obligation to defend my point of view when necessary. I have no right to be truculent, to polarize the group, or to attack other members. Furthermore, I am not compelled to curb my own personal moral commitments or understandings. Still, I cannot be dogmatic; I cannot demand my way and concede nothing to others. Although I know that agreements are generally imperfect, I must do my share in forging agreements. When I am wrong I must concede it, and I must understand that my

ideas may need modification just as much as the ideas of other members. Still, controversy is often useful, and I must respect it and learn from it even though it may take a great deal of time. If we become irrevocably divided, I will recognize that division itself may be an "answer" for us.

I have the obligation to embrace diversity in my group. I know that people are different from me; they have different beliefs, different values, and different attitudes. I will fight against thinking of others as wrong when they do not share my beliefs, attitudes and values. I will strive to keep an open mind at all times so that I can listen to what others say. When I still disagree, I will advance my position politely. I will remain rhetorically sensitive as I speak; I will look to find ways to value the diversity in my group rather than to alienate it.

I know that sometimes groups fail. They fail because individuals get impatient, unreasonable, distracted, or bored. I must take care to avoid these particular "deadly discussion sins." If we do fail, I have the obligation to try to discover what went wrong, but I also know that nothing is gained from accusation and recrimination. We shall simply learn from failure and do better the next time. By the same token, if we succeed I must fight against feelings of overconfidence. Each new group, each new problem, is its own challenge. There is nothing in history or science that will predict the outcome.

And that is the pleasure I take in the process, for I know that I can contribute, and to do so makes me feel more of a human being.

These responsibilities set the stage for all members to work together as a team on a problem that they thoroughly understand. Having successfully completed step one, the members have a solid foundation for group problem-solving.

GOALS

To understand where we are in the process.

- Why are we here?
- What authority do we have?
- What do we have to turn out?
- Who gets it?
- What do they do with it?

OUTCOMES

- Questions about the charge addressed to appropriate persons.
- A written specification of the final task.
- A record of our understanding of the task.

MEMBER TASKS

- To raise questions about the nature of the group task.
- To raise questions about personal responsibility to the group.
- To raise questions to be addressed to higher authorities.
- To raise questions about schedule or agenda.

LEADER OBLIGATIONS

- To raise necessary questions pertinent to understanding the group task.
- To transmit and interpret information from higher authorities.
- To act as liaison between the group and higher authorities.
- To ensure that agreements and understandings of the group are written into the record.

�֍ 8 ֍

Standard Agenda Step Two
Understanding and
Phrasing the Question

A task group was appointed to solve a campus parking problem. Ginny declared, "We need a new parking garage!" Tom thought they needed to do a better job of ticketing illegal parking. "No, No, what we need to do is to incorporate a shuttle bus for the outer parking areas," said Dennis. This group is obviously in trouble. They have skipped to step five of the standard agenda and are already exploring possible solutions thus bypassing an essential step: defining and analyzing the problem. A group cannot effectively solve the problem if they (1) don't fully understand the problem (and what is causing it) and (2) are unaware of variables that can affect the solution. The group needs to fully comprehend all the possible elements of the problem: Who is having the trouble parking? Are they finding remote parking but are just annoyed at the distance they have to walk? What time does the parking "problem" begin? The group members need to understand variables that affect implementing a solution: How much money is the university willing to spend? Is physical space available? It would be a big waste of time to propose a

---

Don't Let This Happen to Your Group

Have you been in groups where members focus immediately on solutions? Did you try to redirect attention to defining the problem thoroughly before attempting to "solve" an issue that might mean one thing to one group member and something entirely different to another?

---

parking garage when the university does not have the budget for it. None of these questions can be answered if the group seeks a solution before considering all the components affecting the current situation.

Becoming solution-centered before the group becomes problem-centered is a real hazard. Although disagreements about solutions can be productive in later phases of discussion, they are seldom useful until the group has agreed on the precise nature of the problem and has formulated a question to guide its deliberations. The primary goal of step two is to accomplish both these tasks, and this chapter will describe how to do it. By taking the time to understand a problem and to generate a question that encourages good inquiry, your group can increase the likelihood that your work will be efficient, productive, and consequently satisfying.

⅋ Goals of Step Two ⅋

Once your group understands your charge, it is time to explore the background of the problem and to word the problem in the form of a question so that:

1. All members understand it in the same way.

2. All members know what problem-solving level they will eventually need to reach:
   - finding facts.
   - evaluating the status quo of a situation.
   - solving a problem.
   - making a decision.
   - laying down a policy

3. All members understand whether they are examining symptoms or causes of the problem or both.

EXPLORING THE BACKGROUND OF THE PROBLEM

Most of the time when we are charged with a task, there is no specific definition of the problem. The boss's supervisor may understand there is something wrong with worker morale, but he or she does not know the details.

To define the problem accurately, your group will need the answers to some or all of these questions:

How did this issue arise?
- Who decided it was a problem?
- Is it the result of routine evaluation?
- Is there an emergency?
- Check the charge for information about the source of the problem.

Is the problem for:
- Workers?
- Bosses?

Did it develop from another issue?
(Sometimes a solution to a problem creates a new problem!)

Is there anyone else working on this problem?

Did someone lodge a complaint?
- Who complained?
- Who got hurt?
- How seriously?
- Single case of injury?

Are we just anticipating trouble?
- Do we have evidence of a potential problem?
- Are we creating drama where none exists?

Has this issue come up before?

- Recurring problem?
- What was done?
- How did it work?

- What other group addressed the issue?
  - government?
  - private citizen groups?
  - another task group in the company?
- What was the effect?
- What can we learn from the experience of others?
- Were the situations similar enough to ours to make a comparison?

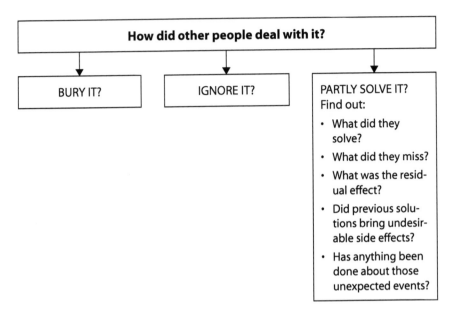

Your group may use any or all of these questions as you see fit. Remember, the goal here is to gather as much background information as possible so that you can better understand the problem. You should refrain from prematurely discussing solutions at this time.

PHRASE THE QUESTION

Once you understand the background of the problem, it is time to phrase the question. The purpose of step two is to make sure every group member understands the problem. If everyone is very clear about the goal, the group can move forward. Wording the question properly can stimulate thinking.

Your question should be specific, realistic, and open-ended to allow for the widest range of inquiry. You do not want the question to polarize the group, lead to debate, or include a solution in the question.

Be Specific

The question must specify who is to act (the subject of the question) about what (the object of the investigation). Questions that start "What are we to do . . .?" imply that the discussion group will take the action. Questions that start with "What is the university to do . . .?" do not specify who, in the university, is to act. The appropriate subject of the question is usually the agency that assigned the project. "What should the president (board of directors) of the university do . . .?"

While the wording of the question may seem insignificant, each slight variation of wording heads the group in a different direction. Your group should not make the mistake of taking this step lightly or hurrying through it.

For example, if your charge is to rank-order candidates in order of preference for hiring, your question might be: "In what preferential order should we rank our candidates to be hired?" The answer to that question is a rank order. If you use "How should we rank the candidates in order to be hired?" the answers are "pull names out of a hat, use criteria, etc." and you are off solving a different problem.

Be Realistic

Consider these two examples:

Poor choice: What should the university do to beat out the opposition in attracting new students next year?

Good choice: What should be our admissions goals for new students next year? or What is one thing we can do to increase the number of applicants and acceptances?

Can you see why the poor example is not realistic? The word "opposition" is unclear and not specific. "Admissions goals" has specific meaning. We can set admission goals and then see by what percentage our new student admissions increase. It is much more realistic to focus on an admissions program than to focus on "beating out" an unspecified entity. You will have no means of measuring whether your plan "beat out" anyone. We can work on our goals, but we do not have control over the methods of others.

Using our discussion from the previous chapter, realistic questions are always easier to focus on:

Poor choice: How can we eliminate racial prejudice?

Good choice: What can we suggest as effective behavior for students at this university to combat racial prejudice?

This question is very clear about who is to do what about what. It is also realistic, and the solution has a potential for implementation.

Use Open Questions

Open questions allow for a wide range of inquiry. Closed questions are answered with a simple yes or no answer:

Closed: Should we do something about housing for the elderly?

Closed: Should we provide apartments or group homes for the elderly?

Open: What advice can our group give to our Congressional representative about House Bill 766 on housing for the elderly?

Closed: Should we meet the students' demands to change graduation requirements?

Open: What graduation requirements should the university senate recommend to the trustees?

You can easily see how the open questions lead to much more discussion and valuable output for the group.

Avoid Questions that Lead to Debate or Beg the Question

What is begging the question? When you beg the question, you are actually proposing a solution by embedding it within the question. By doing this, you limit your ability to examine a wide range of solutions.

An example of begging the question would be:

"How can we increase the number of parking spaces on campus?"

This is also referred to as a "solution" question. The group has already proposed the solution, right in the question: "increase the number of parking spaces." The group may find out that there are actually plenty of spaces on campus already. The problem of people obtaining them may lie in the fact that most of the classes are scheduled between the hours of 9:00 AM and 1:00 PM but your group would never know that if they asked the question in that manner. Their proposal for, let's say, a new parking garage, would end up costing the university a considerable amount of money—and it would go unused for most of the day.

A better question would be:

"What can we do to ensure that each person has a space to park in each day?"

The answer to this question might be a garage, but it also might be a rescheduling of classes to better distribute them throughout the day. A solution is not implied in this question.

Unanswered and Unanswerable Questions

In his book *Levels of Knowing and Existence*, Harry Weinberg suggests a method for attaining precision in phrasing questions. Weinberg makes a distinction between unanswered and unanswerable questions. An unanswered question is one that has an answer, but the question hasn't been asked: "What, if any, mechanical malfunctions contributed to school bus accidents in 2006?" Safety experts and accident reports for 2006 could be consulted concerning bus accidents. Although you might not be able to make determinations for all cases, you could reasonably rely on technical reports to bring you close to an accurate, general answer. This would be an unanswered but answerable question.

Questions like "What is the role of morality in the home in shaping the degree of commitment students make to academic life?" might make for an interesting philosophical discussion, but there are too many words that cannot be linked with real events and occurrences. Moreover, a causal relationship cannot be established with certainty. Even if a group of experts made up questionnaires that purported to measure morality in the home, student commitment, and the various aspects of academic life, there would be considerable argument about "reliability," "validity," "design procedures," and so forth. It would not even be clear where to look for data. The question is unanswerable. We all define morality a little differently.

It would be somewhat more useful to ask, "What is the relationship, if any, between parental encouragement of study and students dropping out of school?" This wording provides at least some specific questions that can be asked of interviewees. On the other hand, the answers to the questions might still be insufficient for generating a policy to deal with school dropouts.

This leads to another conclusion about questions. Just because questions can be answered does not mean that they are necessarily worth asking. Someone might want to investigate how much anxiety baseball fans experience when games are canceled due to rain. Even if the level of anxiety could be measured, what would be the solution? Questions are useful to discussion groups only when they are related to some issue of importance to the group or the organization the group represents.

Make sure that your question (1) refers to your problem as presented in the charge, (2) can be answered, (3) is worth asking, (4) is presently unanswered, and (5) follows the criteria for wording listed above.

> Try it out. Write a sample discussion question for a charge to send five suggestions to your university president. Now try for a charge to recommend ways to combat apathy at your workplace.

TYPES OF QUESTIONS

Once you have worded your question to the group's satisfaction, it is important to determine if it is a question of fact, value, or policy. Understanding this distinction will help you focus in the upcoming steps. You may also find that, after deciding the type of question, your group made a mistake. Do not hesitate to rewrite the question to better suit your problem.

Fact Questions

The simplest possible question is a question of fact, a question that asks to what degree something does or does not exist or what its nature is. "What mental health problems are experienced by students at our university?" and "How was the budget expended last year?" are questions of fact. They produce relatively factual, general conclusions.

Value Questions

Group members must also deal with questions of value. Such questions deal with the issues of "desirability," "value," or "worth" and are often expressed by statements that embrace or reject a particular attitude.

For example, "What would be desirable about the university recruiting students from minority groups?" is a value question because it asks about the desirability of a general course of action. The group would have to gather facts about the proportion of minority students in the school and determine if that level is representative of the general population. They would need to debate the value of a more diverse student body. The advantages of greater diversity would be part of the discussion in order to determine the answer to the question.

There are groups that exist to provide their members with opportunities to share opinions, ideas, and interpretations. Value questions are a major focus in groups that discuss "great books" or "great ideas." Lively discussions and heated exchanges sharpen people's insights or ideas. However, these types of groups do not normally produce the kinds of formal decisions that lead to the solution of problems. Our focus in this book is on purposive, problem-solving group discussion. Value questions do play a role in these groups, particularly as a component in reaching policy decisions.

Value-based questions enter the discussion when fact-finding is complete and the group must decide whether it needs to proceed: "Is this situation serious enough to warrant action?" "What priorities should we assign to the various situations we have discovered in our fact-finding?" "Where should we devote the bulk of our effort and resources?" These are questions that are implicit in all policy-making discussions. In any case, it is useful to stop after fact-finding to make sure that everyone agrees on the gravity of the situation. If the problem is not serious enough to warrant concern, the group is free to stop.

Policy Questions

The type of question that most frequently engages problem-solving groups is the policy question. Questions of policy concern possible actions by some individual, group, agency, or organization—for example, "What action plan can we implement in order to get more students to participate in the pep rallies?" The action can be a decision about some event, it can be the design of a program to remedy some problem, it can be the creation of a set of policy guidelines for an ongoing operation, and it can be a combination of all those things. Groups engaged in solving this type of problem may reach a decision, make a recommendation, or implement a policy.

Essentially, groups addressing a policy question deal with the validity, feasibility, and desirability of courses of action applied to the events or situations that brought the group together in the first place. For example, "What should the Anytown City Council declare as its policy on rezoning area B?" is a policy question because it directs the group to come up with an action plan on the rezoning. If the group asking the question about the desirability of recruiting minorities decides that the university does have some specified responsibility, a policy question can be raised: "What is the best way that the university can recruit students from minority groups?" Discussion of the policy question should be preceded by a fact-finding discussion on the question, "What is the state of recruitment of students from minority groups?"

Most policy questions involve gathering facts. The problem of "rezoning area B" requires a complete survey of the local area and surrounding areas by a group of people hired to do the job. You will find that most policy questions include extensive fact-finding as well as value discussions. In the following section we assume that you are going to deal with questions of policy, but we must also recognize that most of those questions will involve fact-finding and questions of value while assessing goals, programs, and situations.

Research Check

A call for more research. "To date, those interested in studying communication in decision-making and problem-solving groups have restricted their attention primarily to ones discussing questions of policy. What they have learned in the process, however, may well have limited relevance to discussions of other types of questions that require choice and that may, in fact, have considerable impact on what groups addressing questions of policy ultimately decide" (Gouran, 2003, p. 121).

✒ Outcomes of Step Two ✑

By the time you have completed step two, your group should have clarified your charge. You should have a precisely worded and defined discussion question that will guide the rest of your problem-solving experience and keep you focused. You should also understand whether you are facing a problem of fact, value, or policy.

✒ Member Tasks in Step Two ✑

This step is vital. If you fail to understand this stage you may become confused and impede the group's progress later. Most of this step is devoted to testing yourself to see whether your understanding of the question is the same as that of your colleagues. If you seem to be seeing things differently from the others, you have the obligation to speak up. Common understandings are essential at this point.

If every member tries to keep every other member clearly informed while the question is being worded, your group can avoid some major troubles. A careless examination of the background of the question, for example, might lead your group to misunderstand causes and come up with a solution that does not solve the problem or addresses only a portion of it. Furthermore, unless the question is worded in such a way that all understand it, you may find yourself engaged in debate at later stages of the discussion.

If members fail to participate during this phase of discussion, they can contribute to feelings that discussion is a waste of time, that individuals were suppressed, that the group was not always focused, and that individuals sometimes acquiesced to others. Note that each of these difficulties result from individuals ignoring their responsibilities in the stage of formulating the problem question.

You will need to raise questions about the problem, its nature, and its severity. As you listen to others report and comment on the problem, think of what information is missing and from where it could be obtained. By pointing to missing information, you help the group word its problem so that sensible, comprehensive fact-finding is possible. If you are in a classroom group, you may want to ask your instructor to comment on your question.

✂ Leader Obligations in Step Two ✂

We remind leaders of their regular duties: (1) to summarize, (2) to introduce new material, (3) to referee conflicts, (4) to maintain the record, and (5) to move the group ahead. Given the goals, output, and members' obligations for this phase of discussion, obligations of leaders should be clear. Leaders must be particularly careful about keeping their groups centered on problems and not on solutions. They can maintain such a focus by making certain that all group members understand the problem in the same way. It might be useful to review the charge.

Obviously, leaders need to be in command of background information and be aware of the resources available to the group. Leaders who newly emerge from groups may not have time to prepare special background information; they will need to make sure that this information is identified and secured before step two closes. The leader must restrain the group from jumping ahead until the necessary information is available. The leader will need to help the group coordinate all information-gathering efforts and must also see that tasks are parceled out and completed.

When the leader is confident that an adequate understanding of the problem has developed, it is time to formalize agreement on the question. Whoever is leading the group should be skilled in phrasing problem questions in order to incorporate all the members' contributions. The leader may need to be a "consultant," showing the members how to form a good question and making suggestions to stimulate participation from all members.

When the group reaches agreement on the precise phrasing of its question, the leader should remind the recorder to register the question in the record so that the group can move on to the next phase of the standard agenda. The recorder should distribute copies of the problem question, including any necessary definitions and agreements about its meaning and scope.

Now that the first two steps of the standard agenda have been completed, we can turn to the matters of gathering and evaluating information. The next chapter provides guidelines that will enable you to decide what data you need and to evaluate the importance and accuracy of the information you gather.

GOALS

- To agree on the problem.
- To phrase a question specifying the problem that allows the maximum range of possible answers.
- To agree on the type of question.
- To agree on a focus (symptoms or causes).

OUTCOME

- A precisely worded question to guide the group to the most appropriate solution.

MEMBER TASKS

- To raise questions about the nature of the problem.
- To register preliminary attitudes about the nature and severity of the problem.
- To offer information about the history and causes of the problem.
- To point out what information is needed to begin the study of the problem and to offer sources for obtaining it.
- To make proposals about the wording of the question.

LEADER OBLIGATIONS

- To ascertain that all members understand the problem.
- To guide members to tasks they can perform that will equip them to participate in future steps of discussion.
- To make sure the group understands the cause-symptom issue and how it has been resolved.
- To make sure members understand differences among questions of fact, value, and policy, and agree which type of question they will pursue.
- To make sure that group understandings are reflected in the wording of the question.
- To make sure the question is appropriately written into the record.

✺ 9 ✺

Standard Agenda Step Three
Fact-finding

Without adequate information, group discussions are bull sessions at best. However, it takes considerable effort to find the information necessary to conduct an effective discussion. Many groups avoid this step of the standard agenda simply because it is so difficult; others become fatally bogged down in a morass of facts. In this chapter we will show you how to avoid both pitfalls.

✺ Goals of Step Three ✺

In order to completely understand every facet of the problem, group members will:

- Determine whether they are focusing on the symptoms of the problem or the causes of the problem, or both.
- Compile a body of factual material that will help them understand the situation they must resolve.
- Evaluate the information they gather.

GETTING STARTED

A symptom is an indicator of a problem—a sore throat and fever are symptoms of strep throat. Causes are the things that bring about a particular effect or result—bacteria cause strep throat. Evidence is a fact that supports the idea that there is a problem: when your strep test comes back positive, you now have evidence of strep. Another example could be employee apathy. The inability to get workers to attend a workshop would be a symptom of apathy; its cause might be an incompetent or belligerent boss. Your problem solving will take a different path depending on your focus.

Once you decide on your focus, you need to establish a fact-finding plan. You should have a good idea of what you are looking for, where you will look, and who will do the looking. Review the list of member interests and strengths that you generated in step one. You should be able to plan around those interests and strengths. Deciding who will look where for what will help to make sure no one is repeating work done by others. The correct assignment of research tasks makes the process more productive.

If you don't have a plan, and simply collect everything you can find on the topic, it is possible to be overwhelmed with facts. For example, the library of a major university once set up a committee charged with gathering statistics about the university's operations. The result was thousands of unorganized pieces of information. The facts were there, but it was impossible to find anything anyone really needed because the volume of information was so overwhelming.

You should also know why you are doing what you are doing so that you can keep a focus. Another library group decided to do some fact-finding research. They came up with 200 pages of statistics that included such things as the number of books checked out at a particular time of day, the number of times students were caught sneaking books out of the library, and a ranking of popular tables. But nothing ever happened with the data because the group had no goal. The group lacked a reason for data collection.

Successful fact-finding must be a careful process of finding information needed to answer important questions. Each member must participate in figuring out what information is needed, finding it, and evaluating it. Fact-finding cannot be a haphazard process.

BASIC QUESTIONS

To guide your fact-finding efforts, we provide questions that should be addressed as you begin your exploration of the problem. Consistent use of this set of questions in any discussion spares you the indignities of information overload or wandering around libraries wondering what to do.

1. *What are the evidences and symptoms of the problem?*
   - Who reported there was something wrong?
   - On what evidence was the report based?
   - What is happening now that was not happening previously?
   - What is not happening now that was happening previously?
   - Who is complaining about what?

Looking at a more community-centered problem, consider three towns: Corning, Mansfield, and Lawrenceville. A new factory opened in Corning. Most of the workers live in Mansfield. In order to get to work they have to go through Lawrenceville. Downtown Lawrenceville merchants are complaining that traffic is so heavy that people are not able to stop and shop. Factory management is complaining about congestion that keeps workers from getting to their jobs on time. Workers are complaining about the tension of getting to and from work. All in all, it is not a pleasant situation.

2. *What is the effect of these symptoms?*
   - Who is being affected?
   - How serious is it?
   - In what way does it matter?

In our example, virtually everyone is displeased. The citizens of Lawrenceville resent their town being used as a traffic funnel. Workers are upset about travel problems. Travel time affects the quality of their work. Factory managers wonder why they opened the plant in the first place.

3. *Has this ever happened before? If so, how was it handled?*
   - How has the problem been dealt with before in the present locality?
   - In other places?

There never have been traffic problems like this in the area. The tri-towns were sleepy little places where people moved slowly. But downstate, in Williamsport, it became necessary to build a traffic bypass to channel cars from one town to another in a similar situation. The state paid part of the cost.

4. *What caused the condition?*
   - What motivated the people involved to change what they were doing?
   - Why did the company locate in Corning? (Could the tax-rebate program enacted by the Corning town council have anything to do with it?)
   - Why did most of the workers come from Mansfield? (Could the fact that a small Mansfield factory recently went bankrupt have anything to do with it?)

Causes may be easy to find; often, they are hard to remedy. The group will have to make a decision here about whether to concentrate on the traffic problem (symptomatic focus) or to work on the whole economic condition of the region (causal focus).

5. *What have other interested and expert parties had to say about this issue?*

First you must define who qualifies as an expert, and on what. Do you need traffic experts, personnel experts, legislators, regional planners, or all of these?

6. *What might happen if the problem is not addressed?*

It is important to estimate possible consequences. The economic consequences take little imagination to calculate. The factory can pull out. If the factory stays, however, the downtown area of Lawrenceville can be ruined.

7. *In the light of new information, what is our problem now?*

The original broad question may have been "What can the town council of Lawrenceville do about traffic congestion in the downtown area?" Does it warrant changing? Should a regional planning issue be raised? Should the mutual dependency of the tri-towns be studied? Before moving on, the question should be properly revised so the group can work on a manageable problem.

Your group gathers facts in order to proceed. Your search for information may reveal there is no problem or that nothing can be done about what is going on. You may find immediate action is necessary, or you may opt for a long-range program. Sometimes, after gathering information, you will discover the problem you set out to consider is not the real problem at all. New information may clarify your sense of what is happening, and you must modify your question and refocus your search for information. Fact-finding continues until your question is refined and you have enough information to handle your new question. You should not be overly critical; however don't wait for *all* the information, for you will never get it.

We are assuming that you have taken courses that covered where to look for information. You can gain valuable information from library resources, search engines on the Internet, and interviews with experts. If you do not know where to look for information on a research question, you need to make an appointment immediately with an appropriate librarian or resource professional at your university.

To demonstrate how universal the preceding questions are, try to apply them to some simple problems in your college community. Consider problems like the cost of textbooks, availability of academic advisors, the losing soccer team, rising tuition costs, the quality of food in the dining halls, or student health care. Phrase a discussion question and then try to figure out what kinds of information you would have to seek in order to answer it.

CRITERIA FOR EVALUATING INFORMATION

Information comes in various forms. You may have statements of fact, generalizations, definitions, authoritative statements, and reasoned conclusions. Each must be evaluated against the criteria of credibility, competence, currency, relevance, and sufficiency. This is especially important as you examine information on the Internet.

Credibility

If there are valid reasons for believing the information, then the information is credible. A statement is credible if it comes from a believable (unbiased) source, if it can be confirmed (do other sources say the same thing?), and if it is consistent with other information. You must check out any statement that appears unusual or outlandish. For example, if you are investigating sales losses in various regions and you get a report that one salesperson has increased business by 75 percent, it makes good sense to check again for the possibility that inaccurate information was transmitted or unusual circumstances accounted for the unusual fact. In evaluating credibility, you need to examine carefully whether there are biases and prejudices that might exist in information.

If you are getting information from an eyewitness, for example, you must check to see why the person was observing and what the person could actually see. Sometimes eyewitnesses are so startled by what they see that they miss important details. In other cases, eyewitnesses are biased and see only what they wish to see. It is important to confirm eyewitness testimony. Lawyers who try criminal cases will tell you that eyewitness testimony is often unreliable and frequently can be refuted through examination of additional evidence. A witness may see a car swerve left when tire tracks show the car swerved right. In such cases, the physical evidence is more trustworthy.

Competence

The ability of the reporting source to understand what he or she sees is an indication of competence. Untrained personnel can observe technical operations firsthand without having the vaguest notion of what they are seeing. Competent sources are able to understand the details of the event, situation, or process on which they are reporting. For example, a newspaper story incorrectly reported that detectives present at a hostage situation were "unarmed." The reporter simply did not know that plainclothes detectives keep their weapons concealed. Although this is a specialized example, it illustrates that information is not reliable if it does not come from someone who understands the details of what is being observed.

It is important to ask what the source knows. Inquire about a source's level of training, if any, and extent of general knowledge about the situation. A machinist and an engineer will give very different accounts of the state of the equipment. Neither is necessarily wrong, because each has been trained to look at different aspects of the operation. Generally, accountants are more likely to understand financial details and to overlook important aspects of production. Conversely, production engineers will spend little time thinking about costs. Differing perspectives and expertise explain why many different kinds of people are needed in discussion groups.

Currency

Information should be current, or it will not be considered accurate. There is no hard rule on what is considered to be out of date. Mainly, the timeliness of the material depends on the nature of the topic. While a 10-year-old source on the Civil War would be perfectly appropriate, a one-year-old source on the status of the AIDS virus might be terribly out of date. There is ordinarily an abundance of information, but you need to pay attention to its currency. You must always raise questions about whether there is more current information.

Relevance

Relevance is always measured by its relevance "to" something else. Fact-finding groups often find themselves overloaded with high-quality information that has nothing to do with the topic they are investigating. By referring to the list of questions at the beginning of this chapter, you can discover whether an item of information is relevant to your problem solving. If it helps answer those questions, it is relevant to your group. If it does not, file it for possible later use.

Sufficiency

If you have enough information to meet the needs of your discussion question, your information is adequate or sufficient—you know enough to draw conclusions about the problem. However, the process of fact-finding never ends; there is always something new to be learned. On the other hand, to meet the charge, you need to move on to the next phase of discussion as quickly as possible. The following questions should help you make the decision about whether or not you have sufficient information.

- Do you know the evidences and symptoms of the problem? Can you make a statement about what is going on that should not be or what is not happening that should be?

- Do you know who is being hurt and how? Can you estimate the possible consequences if the situation continues? Have you gathered information from representative people who are being injured or who might be affected by solutions to the problem?

- Do you have background on the problem? Do you know when it started and how it progressed? Have you received information directly from people involved in it? Have you examined other attempts to deal with the problem to find out how well they worked and what more needs to be done?

- Have you received information about similar cases? Are you able to argue that the cases are similar?
- Have you received information from authorities representing various points of view? Have you identified the best experts and found out what they think?
- Are you able to set priorities? Do you know how urgent it is to find a solution to the problem?

Once you have enough information to answer these questions, you can decide whether to modify the original question or to keep it. Understanding the facts in the case frequently enables groups to rephrase their questions more specifically. Furthermore, you should be able to decide whether you must deal with symptoms of the problem, modify causes, or deal with both. It is also possible that information gathering may lead a group to conclude that there is no problem.

ADDITIONAL CONSIDERATIONS

Your use of information should follow the principle of *caveat emptor*—let the buyer beware. Here are some additional considerations to guide your assessment:

1. *Not all books are authoritative.* Authorities write books. So do people who are not authorities. Check the source of the publication. A qualified authority is usually published by a reputable house, without obvious bias, and at the publisher's expense. But that does not mean that all authors published in this way are authoritative.

2. *Find out what the authority really knows.* Many years ago, a Nobel Prize winner in physics began issuing statements about genetics. The statements were provocative and drew a great deal of attention. The physicist claimed geneticists were biased against him. On the other hand, experts in genetics claimed the physicist did not know enough to interpret information accurately. There were few corroborating opinions, virtually no corroborating evidence. Be sure your authorities are legitimate experts on the topic they discuss. Check for biases. Be suspicious if an authority expresses ideas to the advantage of those who control his or her salary and advancement. Finally, check specific factual statements. If there are footnotes or references, be sure to check that information is quoted accurately from other sources. Consistent misquotes or inaccurate representation of information by your authority sheds doubt on his or her opinions.

3. *Make sure that your authority assumed the burden of proof.* If your authority's ideas are inconsistent with other information, be sure to examine the evidence on which the statements are based.

When there is an inconsistency, those who express the minority opinion have the obligation to show why their ideas differ from those of established authorities. Louis Pasteur, for example, had to perform several delicate experiments before the French Academy would accept his idea that bacteria caused disease.

4. *Check the reputability and bias of the publishing source when using authoritative or factual statements drawn from abstracts or reports.* Government data is usually reliable, but they are usually presented in overwhelming quantities. You will need to sort through them carefully and make sure you get precisely what you are after. Corporations generally do not misrepresent information in their reports; but, to make themselves look better, they may omit negative data or emphasize material that sheds the best light on the situation.

5. *Check reports of experimental findings or generalizations against similar investigations.* Where possible, the material should be retested. Generalizations drawn from experimental studies, surveys, questionnaires, and systematic observations should legitimately represent the data. Do not accept generalizations without checking the data on which they were based.

6. *When examples are offered, be sure they fit the generalization they are designed to illustrate.* Examples are not proofs in themselves. They clarify or illustrate complicated generalizations. To be effective, they must contain the main elements included in the generalization. If, for instance, you use an example to illustrate the situation of the typical mortgage holder, you must select a case that contains all the elements of typicality. This is often hard to do, for generalizations are averages, and it is virtually impossible to find an "average" family. Some authorities will construct an example to illustrate average. Be alert to the use of hypothetical examples and regard them as explanations, not demonstrations.

7. *Check the credibility of Web pages when using the Internet for research.* How do you know a credible site from a non-credible site? You need to first analyze the address. A ".edu" site is an educational site, a ".gov" site is a government site, a ".org" site is an organizational site, and ".com" can be any number of groups or organizations. Many of these sites contain facts, but they also contain opinions. You might assume the information is accurate, but you need to verify the information before you use it. It would be reasonable to expect the national site on Special Olympics to be accurate. While product sites may offer some facts, the information is shaped to persuade you to believe in the product or the company. If we, the authors, created a university Web site, we would have an address with a ".edu" extension. What if we included medical advice from Dr. Young? No one would regulate this information. It

would be up to you to determine that we are not medical doctors even though we use the title "Dr."

There are some other measures you can take as well. If there is a tilde (~) in the address, it means a subgroup of the original domain has published the site. The original site may not control the information. You should determine the credibility of the person who authored the information. Evaluate whether the information is fact or opinion. How current is the information? Look for a disclaimer on the Web page and consider its significance. There are thousands of Web sites; many are inaccurate. Just because information is on the Internet, doesn't mean it's true.

Using Language

As you progress through fact-finding, carefully analyze the language that you encounter. Be sure to review the difference between denotative and connotative meanings of words. Interesting writing or speaking demands the use of synonyms, which involve shades of difference in meaning. To avoid semantic arguments, you must be aware of how various types of definitions are used.

Dictionary definitions record the historical meaning of a word. Dictionaries are records of how words have been used. For example, the common word "ecology" has these dictionary definitions:

> Ecology 1. The branch of biology dealing with the many relations between organisms and their environment; bionomics. 2. The branch of sociology concerned with the spacing of people and of institutions and their resulting interdependency. 3. A political movement organized to protect or conserve air, bodies of water or particular units of plant or animal life from threats from encroaching industrialism. . . .

Suppose you encountered this phrase in a report: "We are concerned with the ecology of the community." Does this refer to the organisms that live in the community, relationships between community institutions, or political activity on behalf of the environment? To clarify the sentence, the author would need to use an operational definition.

Operational definitions are technical specifications of what a word means in a particular document: "By 'ecology' we refer to the relationship between the company and community institutions with which it comes in contact—for example, police, schools, business organizations, and financial units of government." Operational definitions are used in scientific reports. They specify the conditions of meaning in a particular experiment or study. You must be alert to these types of definitions, for they specify the precise dictionary definitions used. Furthermore, you must be alert to changes in meaning for the same word throughout a document.

✂ Outcomes of Step Three ✂

During this phase of discussion, group members work together to gather and evaluate information. By paying attention to the basic questions we provided at the beginning of this chapter, the group can guide itself through fact-finding so that the problem becomes crystal clear. The more lucidly the problem is stated, the more likely the group can find a suitable solution. The group should have an organized, written record of their facts.

ANSWERING BASIC QUESTIONS

Consider the case of the Planning Commission of the Borough of Lawrenceville. It has been asked by the borough council to come up with a proposal to handle the "downtown traffic problem." The Planning Commission is an advisory body; it cannot pass legislation, but it can prepare legislation for consideration. It can also decide whether legislation is needed to solve a problem or whether some other means can be used. Here are questions considered and the sources consulted.

What Are the Evidences and Symptoms of the Problems?

1. A survey taken by the Chamber of Commerce last year showed that 45 percent of people living in Mansfield and working in Corning reported being late going to or coming from work at least once during the last three months. Residents of the west side of Lawrenceville who work downtown or on the east side complain about being late both morning and evening.

2. The Chamber of Commerce reported it had received at least one complaint from every merchant in the downtown area about delayed shipments and deliveries during the past year. Four of the larger stores presented detailed reports on how their business had been impeded because of delayed deliveries.

3. The chief of police reported he was unable to assign enough personnel to manage traffic during peak periods and still be able to cope with other responsibilities. The chief also reported that ambulances, fire trucks, and other emergency vehicles had to be routed around the downtown area during peak periods. He reported that he, the fire chief, and the supervisor of the emergency room at the local hospital feared the consequences should there be an emergency downtown during a peak traffic period.

4. An analysis of business flow in the downtown area showed a drop in revenue of approximately 2 percent because of customers' inability to reach the stores or to find parking places within reasonable proximity.

What Caused the Conditions?

1. Suburbanites traveling to and from work are forced to pass through downtown. Factories on the outskirts of town all have the same working hours.

2. The blocking of Della Street to make a downtown mall last year cut one major traffic route through the downtown area. The parking and traffic pattern designed to cope with this change appeared inadequate to handle the results.

3. Failure to complete the Route 15 Freeway has forced commuters to use the most congested routes.

4. Campaigns to use public transportation for access to and through downtown have failed, since public transportation also moves slowly, and some industries lie outside the area serviced by public transportation.

What Is the Effect of These Symptoms?

Formal complaints, petitions, and legal actions have been received from three neighborhoods adjacent to the downtown area. Minor traffic accidents in the downtown area have risen 18 percent in the last year. Two major merchants have already moved to peripheral shopping malls, and several report they are making plans to move.

Has This Ever Happened Before? How Was It Handled?

1. The mayor blocked all traffic legislation because of lack of funds to make necessary improvements.

2. The opening of the Della Street Mall in response to merchant pressure was not accompanied by plans to address the new traffic flow.

3. No one anticipated the rapid growth of two of the peripheral industries, which resulted in increased traffic pressure.

4. Traffic had never really been a problem in Lawrenceville. There was no legislation other than speed limits and parking zones.

5. The new one-way street plan had been shelved during the election campaign.

6. Other communities in the region have instituted overall traffic plans. Jamestown instituted a one-way street system to facilitate traffic to peripheral industries. (Jamestown lies on the other side of the industrial zone east of Lawrenceville.) Tioga applied for and received state and federal bypass money and used it to route traffic to the industrial zone. Other towns in the region are suffering from similar traffic problems.

What Might Happen if the Problem Is Not Addressed?

There are rumors about stores planning to close or move from the downtown area. One manufacturer has threatened not to expand his plant because of the problems with the traffic flow.

What Do Experts Say about the Issue?

- The Taxpayer's Association has issued a statement objecting to any new taxation for traffic improvement.
- The city engineer presented a formal report to the council from a consultant hired to evaluate traffic flow. The report was extensive and concluded nothing would improve without significant modification of streets and roadways at considerable cost.

In Light of New Information, What Is Our Problem Now?

The commission redefined its problem as follows: "How can traffic flow be facilitated in downtown Lawrenceville during peak periods with no major expenditure of funds?" The words "facilitated" and "major expenditure of funds" were further specified. "Facilitated" was operationally defined as "return to the traffic rate prior to the opening of the downtown mall." "Major expenditure of funds" meant "no bonding or tax increases."

Planning Commission members used a variety of sources to obtain information. Data on traffic problems are virtually endless. Rather than get bogged down in studies, they concentrated on information about the local scene. They relied on testimony from interested parties, recognizing that though those parties might disagree, the *way* they saw the issue was itself part of the problem.

Later on in the discussion process, it might be necessary to get even more information to support the details of a solution. For the moment, however, the commission is on track, focused on *a* problem, if not *the* problem, and prepared to move to the next step of discussion.

ꝏ Member Tasks in Step Three ꝏ

Group members must be prepared to tap all resources in order to get information. Often the first stop is the Internet. Groups try to use general search engines to locate pertinent information. If you are going to look for data, you must have a list of questions to answer. Only if your search for information is focused and is using the appropriate search tools will you be able to manage the flood of information available to you. Get familiar with the tools that your university offers. Many proprietary data banks, like EbscoHost or Lexis Nexis, are more useful than general search engines. If you do not know what these terms mean, then you need to update your computer skills immediately. Uninformed surfing of the Internet hoping for some inspiration is a highly inefficient, time-consuming activity.

Do not neglect other methods of retrieving information. Libraries have books, periodicals, reports, reference works, and almanacs that may not be available on-line.

Members may also need to do some interviewing in order to get accurate and extensive information. Interviewing is a delicate task, for it requires getting a maximum amount of information in a limited amount of time from a person who is often busy or reluctant to give information. The etiquette of interviewing is important. There are four guidelines you must keep in mind.

1. No one is obliged to answer your questions. Therefore,
   - Call in advance for an appointment.
   - Explain why you need the information.
   - Explain how the person will benefit from cooperating.
   - Offer an estimate of time needed for the interview.
   - Assure protection of confidentiality, if necessary.
   - If possible, provide a transcript so that the interviewee can correct errors.
2. Focus questions on interviewee's area of expertise.
   - Ask only for opinions the interviewee is qualified to express.
   - Don't force the issue.
3. Be courteous.
   - Use a limited time for the interview.
   - Interview at the subject's convenience.
   - Prepare your questions in advance.
   - Ask most important questions first.
   - Don't ask for answers that you already know.
   - Don't bait your subject or refute what he or she says.
   - Just get the information, thank the subject, and leave.
   - Be sure to send a thank-you note. This is a simple courtesy that leaves the door open for future contact.
4. Carefully record answers.
   - Use a tape recorder with the subject's permission.
   - Prepare note sheets to facilitate recording answers.

The fact-finding step of discussion is often the slowest and most tedious. It requires more time from members than any other step. Without a satisfactory fact-finding phase, however, the rest of the group's work is pointless. An accurate description of the problem built from careful fact-finding is the surest way to get an effective solution.

⚒ Leader Obligations in Step Three ⚒

The main task for the leader in step three is to remain patient. Going through the steps of information gathering and evaluating can be time consuming; group members are often tempted to jump ahead to consideration of solutions. Fact-finding always contains a discussion within a discussion on the question, "Where can we get the information we need, and how can we interpret it appropriately?" The leader must keep careful control during this phase to make sure the group handles the logistics of information gathering. The leader usually uses these questions:

1. What information do we need? Why do we need it?
2. Where can we get it?
3. Who will do what (division of labor)?
4. Now that we have a pile of information, what is worth taking seriously?
5. What does it all add up to?
6. Does the information suggest revising the question?

Someone has to keep records and files. Someone else has to make copies of important information. Another member has to survey archives and libraries, and someone has to interview authorities and interested parties. Individual members may gather information, but no one should have a monopoly on the information.

The leader should also enforce quality control. Groups are often confronted with exciting information: rumors, firsthand accounts, or scare stories. It is easy to be caught up in the drama. The leader must constantly dampen excessive excitement and subject each contribution of information to the critical tests required to ensure its reliability. To do this well may mean assuming the role of devil's advocate. By questioning all of the information, the group can make better decisions regarding the factual nature of each statement.

GOALS

- To obtain information about the nature of the problem, its causes, and history
- To obtain information about similar problems at other places at other times
- To reach a decision on whether symptomatic or causal treatment is appropriate
- To revise the discussion question, if necessary

OUTCOMES

- A library of factual information, authoritative statements, and evaluations
- Conclusions about the causes of the problem
- Formal reconsideration of the discussion question
- If appropriate, modification of the discussion question in light of new facts

MEMBER TASKS

- To do necessary research: find facts, authoritative opinions, and other relevant information
- To participate in evaluating reliability and validity of all facts presented
- To participate in identifying causes of the problem
- To participate in the decision about whether symptomatic or causal treatment is necessary
- To participate in reconsideration and rewording of the question, if necessary

LEADER OBLIGATIONS

- Direct and expedite gathering, evaluating, classifying, and storing information and opinion
- Direct and expedite decision about nature of treatment (symptomatic or causal)
- See to it that the discussion question is evaluated and reworded if necessary

✤ 10 ✤

Standard Agenda Step Four
Setting Criteria and Limitations

Although this step is easily bypassed, developing a useful set of criteria is imperative to effective problem solving. At this point, your group may be tempted to jump right into proposing a solution; you think that once the problem has been clearly expressed and the facts have been thoroughly evaluated, it is a simple process to agree on a solution. It is important to understand, however, the variables that can impact the solution. Otherwise, the group may waste time proposing a solution that either is not possible (it exceeds the limitations, i.e. budget) or does not solve the problem. By clarifying what it can and cannot do as well as developing reasonable goals, your group should progress more effectively toward a solution. This is what step four is all about.

✤ Goals of Step Four ✤

In this step, the group should agree on and complete a list of criteria and limitations. The criteria generation process generally consists of three stages:

- Generating the list of the criteria
- Defining the terms in the criteria
- Prioritizing the criteria in order of importance.

Criteria are standards used to judge possible solutions. Think of them as goals: What could be *achieved* by an effective solution to the problem? We all have personal standards we use to judge restaurants, movies, a professional report, a clean house, or a successful applicant. We suggest the wording "Any solution must/should . . ." as a heading for the criteria list. This wording will help you focus on your outcomes. Remember, you are not just trying to choose a solution, you are trying to solve a problem. Therefore, whatever that problem is must be fixed by the solution. Therefore, think about how you will know a good solution when you see it.

> What are your criteria for a good restaurant? In order to be good, a restaurant must. . . .
>
> 1. _____
> 2. _____
> 3. _____

HOW TO DEVELOP CRITERIA

To devise criteria you should review your research with care, make sure you have a clear understanding of superiors' expectations, and consider your own values in relation to the issues at stake. Your fact-finding results are a primary source of criteria. Review your research to discover the major problems or deficiencies. Consider the causes and symptoms of the problem identified in your research to aid in finding the most effective focus. Review the previous attempts to solve the problem so that you do not repeat any previous errors. Now is the time to reexamine your goals and your charge. If you are directly responsible to some other group or individual, then your recommendations must be acceptable to that person or group. If you are an independent unit, then your solution must be one you are capable of implementing yourselves. If your charge includes specifications of deadlines or budget, these limitations must be observed and stated in your solutions.

Once you have reviewed the information from the previous step, you can generate your list of criteria. The criteria for the Lawrenceville traffic group flowed out of their fact-finding. The facts in the case suggested the criteria and limitations: they could not count on federal funds to help them; some merchants were abusing the issue and making threats for personal advantage; and the community needed the jobs provided by the manufacturer so it was necessary to satisfy the employer. Lawrenceville could have acted without recognizing the needs of the other two counties, but the group recognized that they needed to cooperate with the other counties affected by any decision. They also realized that something needed to change right away, since hostilities were rising. Therefore, they came up with the following six criteria:

1. Any viable solution must allow for speedy transit of deliveries and personnel to and from factories.
2. Any solution should involve the other towns logistically and financially.
3. Any solution should tangibly improve the situation of the merchants who are suffering loss of business.
4. Any solution must be implemented within 2 months.
5. Any solution must fit within the cities' budgets.
6. Any solution must resolve the current hostility and morale problem.

Note that these statements are *not* solutions. A solution is an action statement that directs someone to do something specific; criteria are guidelines for what a possible solution should achieve. They are specifications for building solutions. Criteria specify the desirable part of the formula.

Focusing on a good set of criteria also increases the likelihood that members can reach agreement on solutions when the time comes. If the criteria step is bypassed, there is no order in the decision-making process. As another example, if three faculty members comprise a committee to select the outstanding senior, they would collect all of the facts (through resumes, interviews, or applications). If they jumped immediately to the solution (selecting the person), they might argue for the person they liked the most in interviews, the one who has the highest G.P.A., or the one who has done the most service for the department. By selecting criteria for the solution ahead of time, they are in agreement about what are the most important criteria for judgment before even looking at the candidates; therefore, the problem-solving process is much more systematic, fair, and effective. If an applicant did not get the award, the committee could explain why without hesitation. Their decision was based on developed criteria.

If the committee decided on criteria for selecting the outstanding senior, they might look like this:

1. Any applicant must have at least a 3.50 G.P.A.
2. Any applicant should have performed service to their department.
3. Any applicant should have participated in some kind of scholarly activity (presenting a paper, publishing a poem, etc.).
4. Any applicant should have demonstrated leadership qualities.
5. Any applicant should submit a formal, professionally formatted application.

DEFINING THE TERMS

The next step is to define the terms in the criteria. Misunderstandings often take place when there is not a common understanding of definitions. In the case of the outstanding senior committee, the committee defined the term scholarly activity and gave an actual G.P.A. cutoff. They may find, during the next step, that other terms are ambiguous, for example, what constitutes "service" to the department? Some services would be easy to identify: developing a Web page for the department or speaking to incoming majors. But does the committee want to count filing papers in a departmental office as "service"?

Try to identify two or three ways that this committee could define the term "leadership qualities" that would help to clarify their discussion.

1._____

2._____

3._____

Similarly, the Lawrenceville group needs to define the terms used. What is "speedy transit" or "tangible improvement?" Many of the terms in their criteria are vague and need to be specifically defined before the group moves on.

PRIORITIZING CRITERIA

Once you have generated your criteria, it is important to rank them in the order of importance. The ranking will help in a case where, for example, five criteria for a solution have been generated, and each of two solutions meet three of the criteria. It will be evident which solution is better based on the ranking of the criteria. Consider two students selecting a new bank. For Javon, the location is of the utmost importance. He doesn't care so much about service fees because his parents pay for that. However, he has no transportation, so he could not get to a bank that was not within walking distance. Oksana, on the other hand, has very little income. She is extremely concerned with the service charges and fees. She has a bike and is physically active, so the distance is not a concern for her. Both of these students may use the same list of criteria, but because of their priorities they will probably choose different banks.

Let's return to the outstanding senior evaluation. It is quite possible that two students will meet the same number of criteria. If Mary meets criteria 1 and 3, but Na'eem meets criteria 2 and 3, who will win the award? The committee must prioritize the criteria in order to save time making the decision. They may decide that criteria 2 and 3 are more important than 1. The group can now rank each candidate based on objective and unanimous reasons. Personal issues, loyalties, and political considerations are not part of the criteria.

Your group should use rational thought to decide how to prioritize the criteria. This prioritization can often mean a big difference in the decision. The Lawrenceville group spent numerous meetings on this step alone. In the end, they decided on the following order:

1. Any viable solution must allow for speedy transit of deliveries and personnel to and from factories.
2. Any solution must fit within the cities' budgets.
3. Any solution must be implemented within 2 months.
4. Any solution must resolve the current hostility and morale problem.
5. Any solution should tangibly improve the situation of the merchants who are suffering loss of business.
6. Any solution should involve the other towns logistically and financially.

Can you generate some of the reasons the group would have used to reach the prioritization of these criteria?

1. _____

2. _____

3. _____

Once you are finished generating, defining, and prioritizing the criteria, you can move on to developing the limitations for the group.

How to Determine Limitations

Criteria define what you want to achieve with your solution. Limitations, on the other hand, remind you of what you cannot do. *Limitations* are restraints under which the group operates. They are limits on either the solution or the group. We recommend the wording, "Any solution must not . . ." or "Our group cannot . . ." be the initial phrase for all statements. All groups are limited in various ways, and all problems must be solved within certain constraints. Some limitations include legal restrictions, institutional policies, financial restrictions, and persuasive restrictions.

Legal Restrictions

Solutions should not violate laws. Governmental agencies, colleges and universities, labor unions, and businesses employ legal counsel to examine committee recommendations prior to sending them to agencies responsible for implementation. The legal counselors check to make sure the proposals in no way conflict with existing laws. In some cases, legal limitations interfere with criteria set by groups. For instance, the most economical solution for building a community recreation center (a criterion) may violate zoning ordinances (a limitation), so a less economical plan must be recommended.

Institutional Policies and Traditions

Any viable solution must be consistent with both the formal and the informal codes of the institutions that will be affected. Suppose your company charges a task force with negotiating a medical insurance policy. The best coverage for the least cost is from an insurer that refuses to provide coverage for 8 percent of the company's employees whose work is high-risk. Will you generate a separate policy for these special cases, exclude them from coverage, or recommend a less cost-efficient insurer that will cover all employees? Your choice may be limited by company policies that ban special treatment. It is most important to discover what institutional policies and norms potentially limit your recommendations.

Financial Limitations

Everything costs money. Members of groups pay for beverages, paper, pens, duplication of important documents and findings, transportation costs to and from the meetings, and so forth. Some groups might pay for professional formatting for final reports. Most student groups must rely on member contributions, so it is legitimate and realistic to determine how much money is available to implement solutions. Leaders should take some initiative in seeking funding from charging authorities when such a request is appropriate. When a group is self-charged, members may be able to exercise some imagination in finding sources of funding or in developing strategies.

Persuasive Power

A group has limited persuasive power. Some groups have persuasive power by virtue of their position in the community or organization. Some have persuasive power by virtue of their title. Other groups have no power and must work to win support. To develop persuasive power, establish goodwill and credibility by employing professional interviewing techniques, sending thank-you letters to resource people, and demonstrating how the interests of your group are tied to those of other individuals and groups. To the extent that your solutions receive even informal backing from the powers that be, you increase the probability of success.

Careful attention to limitations in step four may spare the group difficulty, disappointment, or embarrassment later on. In some cases, of course, it is possible to overcome limitations. You may be able to get a law repealed, gain an exception to an existing policy, or petition for an increase in budget. In general, however, it is not a good idea to count on such good fortune. Be prepared to operate within the limitations that exist.

Limitations recognized by the Lawrenceville group include:

1. A solution cannot exceed in cost what the community can raise without bonds and taxes.

2. A solution cannot infringe on laws regarding freedom of trade.

3. A solution must be limited to recommendation, since the group is not empowered to make policy.

Each of these statements clarifies the group's scope of authority and the boundaries within which it must operate.

At this point, your members might ask, "Why bother? Surely most people understand these things without having to talk them through in detail." Most people, however, do not understand criteria and limits. This can lead to trouble. If you proceed in the problem-solving process without a clear plan and understanding of criteria and limitations, you'll spend a much longer time arguing about these specific instances as they come up.

Keep in mind that limitations can be basic and simple or lengthy and complex. For example, the outstanding senior committee may have minimal limitations:

1. We cannot exclude anyone because of race, age, sex, or sexual orientation (the law provides this guideline).

2. We do not have the authority to select the outstanding senior. We only have the authority to make a recommendation.

3. We cannot spend more than two hours on this decision.

Establishing criteria and limitations before discussing solutions increases the likelihood that a group will be able to arrive at a genuine and well-reasoned consensus.

⅔ Outcomes for Step Four ⅗

At the conclusion of this step, you should have two documents before you: (1) a list of criteria for judging possible solutions that includes definitions and is ranked by importance, and (2) a set of limitations within which members understand they must operate. Each member should have a copy of these documents. Once your group agrees on the criteria and limitations, selecting the best solution becomes a logical, rational process.

⚡ Member Tasks in Step Four ⚡

Essentially, step four involves reviewing and addressing the implications of what has been accomplished. It is particularly important to listen carefully and critically, to ask questions to clarify points, to assert your own perceptions of criteria and limitations, and to communicate in ways that consistently keep the focus on collective goals.

You also must stay focused on the charge. It is easy to let your personal views get in the way as you develop and prioritize criteria. Sometimes members will develop criteria specifically to fit the solution that they would like to see implemented. This activity subverts the problem-solving process. An effective group member will try not to let personal preferences interfere with good group problem solving.

> Consider the case of the Outstanding Senior Selection Committee. After receiving nominations from each department based on academic record, leadership, and service, the committee narrowed the list to the top 5 through group discussion based on those criteria. However, after they interviewed the 5 candidates, the members did not want to be bound by those criteria. Instead, each member ranked the candidates based on their own personal criteria rather than on the criteria previously established. The rankings were then averaged together to get the winner. What are the advantages of this plan? Disadvantages? Is this group effective in selecting the student who is truly the most outstanding?

Participation is critical. It might help to have all group members prepare a list of criteria and limitations prior to the meeting. This method provides the group with a broad range of independently generated ideas. The possibility of groupthink is minimized because there are so many ideas, and the goal of comprehensive analysis is maximized.

During this step, members should critically analyze ideas, and the discussion should be thorough. Recognizing and discussing differences is vital to effective problem solving. If disagreements do not take place, your group may find that they overlook some important information. Think of the "bottom line." Reservations about evaluations or omissions must be shared. Understanding the greater issues can help prevent the group from agreeing on solutions that would make the problem worse instead of solving it.

Above all, members should insist on a thorough discussion of criteria and limitations and encourage each other to participate fully and thoughtfully. It is easy to be impatient and to be tempted to rush through these issues in order to get on with solutions. Yet this can be counterproductive in terms of the overall goals of the group. Good questions, attentive listening and response, and enthusiasm for the topics help generate the kind of atmosphere conducive to thorough work.

ᔥ Leader Obligations in Step Four ᔥ

As always, a leader is responsible for summarizing deliberations, refereeing disagreements, maintaining the record, and keeping the group focused on pertinent issues. During step four, much of the leader's work parallels that of the members. A leader should encourage full and balanced participation, should model good listening habits, and should demonstrate enthusiasm both for the topics of step four and for constructive disagreements over issues.

Leaders need to be alert to the possibility of a "wish list" that is simply not feasible. A leader should encourage members to generate realistic criteria and inform members of limitations imposed by superiors. The leader is responsible for making sure that all members recognize the unalterable restrictions within which they must operate.

The leader may also need to direct the group to return to previous stages. If generation of criteria exposes a new issue, the group must obtain related background material and more fact-finding is in order. Members are often reluctant to backtrack and may feel demoralized by the necessity to do so. But problem solving, even with an agenda, is not a strictly linear process. The leader may need to supply motivation and persuade the members that the detour is essential to the group's long-range collective goals.

To clarify limitations, the leader may need to make special assignments during this step; members may be asked to secure additional information on legal issues, economic plans, or institutional practices. When members are asked to perform special duties, the leader should make sure they are recognized for their efforts on behalf of the group.

Finally, the leader should prepare or delegate the final list of criteria and limitations. Copies of this list should be given to all members to enhance the probability of informed participation in the upcoming discussion of solutions.

GOALS

- To identify the moral and legal authority of the group (institutional, logistical, and persuasive limitations on the group)
- To develop standards against which to test proposed solutions

OUTCOMES

- A list of criteria for testing solutions
- A list of limitations on group recommendations

MEMBER TASKS

- To discuss the constraints limiting the authority of the group
- To suggest and develop suggestions for standards that will help the group test solutions
- To participate in reviewing or reworking previous steps in the agenda if necessary to generate criteria and limitations

LEADER OBLIGATIONS

- To consult external authorities regarding limitations
- To make sure the group understands its limitations and enters them in the group record
- To decide whether the group needs to review or rework previous steps in order to manage this step effectively
- To work with members to generate and enter into the record a set of criteria against which solutions can be measured

✗ 11 ✗

Standard Agenda Step Five
Discovering and Selecting Solutions

The goal in this step is to select the best solution. Because effective discussion is an orderly, reflective enterprise, the group should review the criteria established in step four before proposing the first solution. Once the means of evaluating solutions is clearly established, the group must generate as many possible solutions as they can. The purpose of doing this is to have as great a variety of solutions as possible from which to choose. Many groups pick the first solution and implement it, only to find out later that it did not meet the criteria or solve the problem. The broader the range of potential solutions and the more effectively the ideas are evaluated, the better the chances that your group will reach the best possible solution.

✗ Goals of Step Five ✗

There are four essential parts to step five. Your group should carefully consider each of the following:

- Brainstorm a list of potential solutions.
- Evaluate each of the solutions against the list of criteria generated in step four.
- Determine which solution matches the criteria most effectively.
- Create an implementation plan for that solution.

BRAINSTORMING

If there are not a lot of alternative solutions, your group can generate more by brainstorming. Brainstorming is a process in which members propose an unedited stream of thoughts/ideas. This process was introduced during the group dynamics movement of the 1950s. Members can be humorous and imaginative as they follow the rules:

- Anyone can offer any solution, no matter how bizarre.
- Every proposal is written down.
- No one may criticize ideas during the proposal-making period.
- The goal is to get a large quantity of ideas.

There are some drawbacks to brainstorming. Sometimes groups get carried away with the idea of creating an outlandish solution—creativity and originality are not necessarily signs of a good solution. In addition, brainstorming tends to exclude shy members who have difficulty participating in such a lively, extroverted process. Brainstorming is probably best reserved for times when groups seem irrevocably blocked and need to enhance their creativity.

Research Check

An interesting note on creativity—some people are better at it than others, and creative ability seems to be linked to the concept of cognitive closure. "The need for (nonspecific) cognitive closure has been defined as a desire for a definite answer to a question, any firm answer, rather than uncertainty, confusion or ambiguity" (Kruglanski, 1989 cited in Chirumbolo, Mannetti, Pierro, Areni, & Kruglanski, 2005, p. 61). "The results of the current study support the notion that the need for cognitive closure exerts an adverse effect on creativity in groups. Specifically, groups composed of individuals high (vs. low) in need for closure revealed a lower degree of productivity across multiple measures of group creativity. High (vs. low) need-for-closure groups exhibited significantly lesser fluency of ideas. In addition, high (vs. low) need-for-closure groups generated products rated as less creative, original, and innovative by external judges. Finally, high (vs. low) need-for-closure groups exhibited lesser elaboration of ideas" (p 75).

However, brainstorming can also ensure that the group has plenty of solutions to examine.

The Lawrenceville group was able to brainstorm the following solutions:

1. Do nothing and let the businesses move.
2. Build a downtown parking garage with a local loop bus service.

3. Implement a one-way street traffic plan to get double lanes heading through town.

4. Ask employers to stagger work hours so people can travel at different times

5. Seek a government grant for a bypass.

6. Create a community-wide carpool program.

EVALUATING SOLUTIONS AGAINST CRITERIA

At this point, the group is usually excited to choose the solution to the problem (a suggestion, an event, a policy statement, or reasoned decision) complete with arguments for its adoption, a budget where necessary, and a method of evaluating it once it is put into operation. Unfortunately, by the time this phase of discussion is reached, the group is also often fatigued. There is a tendency to jump to conclusions with the phrase, "Well, it's obvious what we ought to do is. . . ." Statements like this obstruct critical thinking and subvert the group's work.

Instead of immediately accepting the first idea, the group should use the criteria generated in step four. If the group subjects an idea to careful scrutiny by testing it against the criteria, they often find that it was not such a good idea. People wonder how they could have been so foolish. Some of the statements that indicate a premature decision are these:

• Well, it looks like we should . . .

• We've got to stop . . .

• Everyone knows we ought to . . .

• It seems apparent that . . .

At this phase of the discussion, nothing is obvious, and nothing should be ruled out.

Evaluating in a systematic manner can take many forms. For beginners, we recommend taking the time to draw up an evaluation sheet that will guide the group members through systematic discussion. The Lawrenceville Planning Commission had a sheet that looked like this:

Solutions: ➡	Do Nothing/ Businesses Move	Parking Garage	One-Way Traffic Plan	Stagger Work Hours	Govern-ment Money	Community-Wide-Carpool
Criteria (Any solution must): ⬇						
Allow speedy transit	Y	Y	Y—?	Y	Y	Y
Fit within budget	Y	N	Y—?	Y	?	Y
Be implemented in 2 months	Y	N	Maybe	Y	N	Y
Resolve hostility and morale	N	Y	Y	N	Y	Y—?
Improve merchants' situation	N	Y	Y	N	N	Y
Involve the other towns	N	N	N	Y	Y	Y

The group then tested each of the proposals against the criteria and limitations. It is imperative to test the solutions against the criteria in a systematic manner. To be effective, the group takes solution #1 and discusses how well it meets criterion #1, then #2, etc. Or the group can see how well each solution matches criterion #1. The group should discuss even the obvious, keeping lots of notes on the discussion, and reasons that a solution meets or does not meet each criterion. Minutes can be mandatory depending on the scope and importance of your problem. The LPC spent hours developing the evaluations above. They were unsure about whether the one-way traffic plan would really speed up the traffic flow. They also needed to make phone calls to get estimates on the cost for changing the traffic signs, etc. They were perceptive enough to realize that the merchants would be unhappy with changing their work hours—that would have the downtown opening and closing at all different hours. They also knew that the workers wouldn't be happy with those changes as well. They questioned whether the workers would be willing to carpool, or if that would create further hostility. After conducting some focus-group research, they found that with the rapidly rising gas prices, most of the workers were actually relieved at the idea of a city-organized carpool. Are there any ratings that the LPC commission decided on above with which you would argue?

SELECTING THE BEST SOLUTION

Once the evaluation phase is complete, the group can select the best solution. It is rare when a group finds a good proposal in complete form. Usually groups put together bits and pieces of various solutions to make the most ideal recommendation. In the case of the LPC, the proposal to do nothing or to build the parking garage were rejected because they did not meet three of the proposed criteria. Staggering working hours and waiting for possible government money were also eliminated because of problems meeting some important criteria. The one-way traffic plan was a possibility, but the LPC saw that the community-wide carpool program might actually meet all of their criteria.

If the solution is not this obvious, once the solution list is reduced to a manageable few, you may want to refine your analysis. You might consider having each person write an anonymous position paper in which they present arguments both for and against a particular proposal. This activity will ensure that sufficient attention is devoted to each proposal. Printed copies should be distributed to all members. Position papers often require a recess of several days to allow members time to think and write.

Here are some questions to guide the writing:

1. What would the proposal cost? Would it meet cost-benefit standards?

2. Who might be injured by the proposal? What is the nature of the injury? Is compensation possible? Is there any way to reconcile people who might be harmed because of the proposal?

3. Are there unanticipated political barriers to the proposal?

4. What are the main advantages of the idea? How important are these advantages? Does their benefit outweigh projected costs? (Costs include not only money, but time and resources as well.)

5. If the position paper advocates a proposal, it should demonstrate how the proposal satisfies the group goals and fits within the imposed limitations.

Intense deliberation and argument is desirable at this point. Because your final report must include a defense, the debate will help you decide what needs to be defended.

In situations where consensus does not seem likely, you cannot postpone decisions indefinitely. Most groups have deadlines and would not be in existence if there were not some important reason for producing a solution in a given time frame. In these cases, it may be necessary to use a less than ideal method to resolve the decision. Although voting has the potential to polarize the group, it is efficient. If your group has a 50–50 split, you may want to spend more time examining proposals. However, if you have a preponderance of opinion on one side, you may determine the most efficient route is to proceed. Unanimity does not just happen; it requires careful and painstaking work to accomplish. If the preliminary four steps were followed as suggested, the group should have explored a sufficient number of avenues that voting will yield a workable solution.

IMPLEMENTATION PLAN

How do you know you are right? The answer is easy: you don't. The group never knows whether it is right until the solution has been implemented and tested. Just because seven or eight people agree on a solution does not mean that it is the best solution or that it is even workable. You must carefully examine the details and potential impact of the solution. Consider, for example, the problems besetting Social Security because longevity was not considered.

Your group should prepare a detailed *implementation plan and budget*; once that is complete, set up an evaluation procedure. This may help the group recognize some easily overlooked details. An operations plan contains the following components:

1. *A general description of the proposal, usually as a heading:*

   Proposal for a Community-wide Carpool Program
   The following proposal seeks to establish a central office to arrange carpooling for workers regularly passing through the downtown area of Lawrenceville.

2. *Personnel involved in the program and their duties:*

   The position of carpool supervisor will be created in the borough hall; a secretary will be assigned part-time. The supervisor will take calls and refer the caller to people in the same neighborhood who would be possible candidates for carpooling. The supervisor will attempt to persuade companies to arrange in-plant pools. The secretary will keep records and handle correspondence as directed.

3. *A statement of resources needed:*

   The solution will require a desk, regular office supplies, a file cabinet, a basic computer and printer, and a phone. There should be office space designated in borough hall.

4. *A statement of supervision and responsibility:*

   A member of the Planning Commission, designated by the Planning Commission, will supervise.

5. *A method of evaluation:*

   The traffic survey committee reports regularly on traffic flow. The program will be considered successful if traffic is reduced 10 percent and/or there is evidence of at least 250 carpools at the end of 60 days.

6. *A tentative budget:*

Costs include salary for carpool supervisor, allotment for part-time support staff, and costs of office supplies and phone. Office furniture and space will be provided by the borough at no charge. Merchants will be asked to fund advertising for the program. (Note that actual cost estimates would be included here.)

Working on the budget is very important. It will raise intriguing questions. Your group must be able to generate a list of each and every expense that will be incurred as well as an estimate for each expense. Here are some of the things that came up during examination of the budget.

- "How will people hear about the program? How will it be advertised, considering we have agreed on minimum expenditure?"
- "Who will benefit? The downtown merchants, of course. Why not get them to fund advertising for it?"
- "OK, but who will go to them to solicit their support? And what if they don't want to fund it?"
- "Well, to blazes with them! If they don't like what we are doing for them, they don't. . . ."
- "Hold it! Maybe we ought to take the time to solicit their ideas before we get carried away."

The budgeting procedure revealed a possible flaw in the solution that required more investigation before putting it into operation. Groups will frequently find a number of reasons to pause during development of solutions in order to test reaction and to get more information about implementation.

This is an extremely brief example of an operations plan. A true plan will be numerous pages in length with plenty of detail and citations.

✺ Outcomes of Step Five ✺

At the close of step five, a group should have a great deal of information. The group should have a set of proposals with reasons for acceptance and rejection. For each rejected proposal, your group should provide a written explanation of why the proposal failed to fit the group's criteria and limits. This document will be used to defend the solution that will eventually be proposed. A well-prepared group will be able to state what was considered and offer reasons why each rejected solution was not accepted. If there is a substantial secondary proposal, it can be included with the final report.

❧ Member Tasks in Step Five ❧

During this step members can find themselves passionate about specific ideas; they can turn into advocates. To be an effective member, you must take care to express your ideas in a way that encourages reflection. The following rules serve as a reminder of member obligations:

1. If you make a statement, you are required to support it. If you offer information, you must document it. If you offer an opinion, you have the burden of proof.

2. If you disagree, you must base your disagreement on something more than personal feeling. You must be able to show why the proposal may not meet the goals, violates the limitations, or will bring unforeseen, unpleasant consequences.

3. When you object, you must focus your objections on the ideas, not on the person presenting them. However, if you are questioning the statements of some outside authority, you may question his or her credentials, objectivity, or interest in the outcome.

4. If you offer a criticism, you should be able to state the standards on which your criticism is based. If you say a proposal will cost "too much money," you should be able to answer the question "how much is too much?" If you say a proposal is "impractical," you should be able to specify some standards for practicality and why the proposal does not meet them. Simply saying "It won't work" or "I don't like it" is not enough.

5. If you ask a question, you should be able to show how the answer is relevant. Sometimes members ask irrelevant questions in order to trap another member or to discredit his or her ideas. Questions should be relevant to the case. This caution, however, does not change the fact that relevant questions *must* be asked. Don't sit back with confidence that someone else will ask what you want to ask. You may be the only person to have a particular idea, and your idea could be very important to the group. It is terribly disruptive to a group to have to go back and answer questions that should have been asked earlier.

6. Keep contributions brief and clear. There are rare moments in discussion when a person may have to function as a technical expert, but most of the time limited contributions and turn-taking are important to facilitate the give and take of constructive discussion. When one person is functioning as an expert, be sure to ask questions if you need clarification. The discussion process rarely requires a lecture.

7. Focus on group goals. It is possible to get a feeling of personal victory if your ideas are chosen over those of others, but this is an example of destructive conflict. Remember to focus on the group goals. Everyone must understand that they cannot get all that they want and must give a little in order to get a little.

Your group should also work to avoid two tendencies during proposal making: unwillingness to try anything new and groupthink. Many groups seem to freeze at proposal time. They tend to propose more of the same old solutions to problems, but any program has a point of diminishing returns. If a one-way street pattern has partially solved a traffic problem, there is no assurance that more one-way streets will solve the rest of it.

Also, by this time, groups may get concerned about getting along with one another. If you avoid argument and critical evaluation, then groupthink is likely to happen. Consensus is sometimes nothing more than a result of fatigue or apathy, so be skeptical of agreement reached too easily. As mentioned in chapter 6, appoint someone as an official devil's advocate if groupthink becomes apparent. This process virtually guarantees that critical questions will be asked.

✄ Leader Obligations in Step Five ✄

Some additional challenges may present themselves in step five. Factions may have formed, and there may be a history of hostility between particular members. Some members may have formed friendships, while others may feel socially excluded. Some may be impatient and others overly sensitive. There are many reasons why individual members may be testy and edgy during this step.

We have been reminding you continually of the leader's regular obligations: to "direct traffic," to provide summaries, and to try to resolve conflict. In this step the leader must also attend to the content of the discussion as well as the process, for it is the leader's job to see to it that the group solution meets the requirements of the charge. The leader responsibilities are outlined below.

1. Stop premature commitment. If members agree too quickly, stop them and raise questions. They may be right, but you cannot be sure until you subject all alternatives to scrutiny and test.

2. Fight fatigue. Take time for refreshment and contemplation. You may be working against the clock, but a marathon effort may be self-defeating. Sometimes it pays to put work aside briefly and to come back to it with a refreshed approach, often resulting in a new perspective.

3. Assign tasks. You may have to direct members to perform certain tasks. You cannot work around a lack of information. At this point in the process, most members will not be volunteering readily. You will need to delegate and to take responsibility for task accomplishment.

4. Maintain contact with the recorder. Your group is discussing considerable detail at this point in the process. Make sure that the recorder is doing an accurate job of keeping track of those details. Refer to the record so that the same issues are not being covered more than once, and review the notes for information you may have missed.

5. Wrap it up. The most difficult task here is stating the final solution. It is important to know when to quit. To do that, you will need to know when consensus is working, when to do some bargaining, and when to take a vote. If you have one dissenter holding out when the rest of the group agrees, you may want to try to please him/her by considering his/her ideas. However, if the ideas have been considered and the person is holding out, then you may need to vote and get on with business. Sometimes several people seem irritated over small issues. That is the time to struggle on consensus on major issues and leave the trivial business to be worked out during the preparation of the final report. Try to avoid a solution so diluted with compromise that it will not work.

Be sure to take time to commend your members for the work they have done. Leaving your members with a feeling of goodwill in this step establishes trust and provides a foundation for future collaboration.

GOALS

- To generate and examine as many alternatives as possible
- To carefully evaluate each solution against the criteria
- To select or construct a solution
- To prepare a plan for operationalizing the solution

OUTCOMES

- A set of proposals with reasons for rejections
- Detail of a proposal with rationale for each component (budget where required)
- Operations plan, complete with method of evaluation

MEMBER TASKS

- To review facts, criteria, and limitations to find, evaluate, and propose solutions
- To participate in constructing a group solution, including operations plan and rationale

LEADER OBLIGATIONS

- To use whatever methods necessary to increase the number of possible solutions to consider
- To guide the group through the process of evaluation of proposals against criteria and limitations
- To supervise development of operations plan, budget, and evaluation procedure

❧ 12 ❧

Standard Agenda Step Six
Preparing and Presenting
the Final Report

In the final step, the group changes its purpose and its method of operation from gathering and analyzing to developing a final report according to the specifications of the charge and the charging authority. Members must accept tasks as assigned by the leader. The leader is actually an administrator coordinating the work of several people in order to accomplish the required task: reporting the group's findings.

In some cases, groups have the authority to implement their own decisions and therefore can move directly to developing an action plan. In other cases, groups submit their decision to someone else who makes the implementation decision. It is essential that your group write an effective report on your proposal and use a skilled speaker if the presentation will be delivered orally. Many fine solutions have been lost in the shuffle because they did not receive an effective, persuasive oral or written presentation in the final report.

As you design your final report, it is important to keep your audience in mind. Most organizations resist change, so if you are expecting your audience to embrace your recommendation immediately, you may be disappointed. It may be wise to assume that you will have a hostile audience. In doing so, you will strive to give your solution the best possible defense—increasing your reports' chances of acceptance. It generally takes a lot of effort to persuade people to adopt a solution, especially if they are obligated to take responsibility should the plan fail.

❧ Goals of Step Six ❧

The goals of step six are to prepare a final report and presentation that clearly articulate your solution. To do this you will need to decide:

- How to write the report.
- What sections need to go into the report.
- What kind of presentation you need to design.
- How you will put it all together.

PREPARING THE FINAL REPORT

You need some initial planning as you begin your report. Will it be informative or persuasive? In the case where you have been asked to rank some candidates, you may simply need to report, in informative style, your actual rankings and the reasoning for each candidate's position. If you have to present a solution to a problem, however, a persuasive report may be more effective. For example, the LPC knew that there might be some initial hesitation to the community-wide carpool program. Their audience (the town council) had a reputation for being argumentative and jumping to conclusions before having all the facts. The LPC felt that the report needed to follow a strict problem-solution format in order to build up to their recommendation.

Writing the Report

As you write this report, your strategy is important. Many groups simply divide the information and each group member writes a section of the report. Your group should be aware that there are many problems inherent with this strategy. First, the writing skills of group members usually vary. Therefore, some sections will be written well, while others will be confusing. Second, each person has his/her own writing style. When someone reads the report as a whole, those style shifts can become annoying and distracting. Third, group members occasionally do not do their work. If a group member does not finish his/her section, then the entire group is in a bind. Finally, if using the section strategy, the report will require extensive editing to correct errors and to achieve a readable flow. Unfortunately most groups are pressed for time at the end of projects. There is a tendency to rush the written report, which creates substandard results. You don't want this to happen after working for a long time on a project.

So how does a group accomplish the written report? We have seen many groups designate a writer or co-writers for the report. Usually this is someone who had a lighter load earlier in the project. If you use only one or two writers, it is imperative that the other group members be available to sit around the computer to offer ideas, suggestions, moral support, snacks, etc.

As one writer completes the rough draft, another person can begin the initial editing. Having two or three people involved in multiple revisions almost always guarantees a tighter, more professional report. When your group thinks that the report is complete, have another person, who is not in the group, proofread the work for errors or unclear wording.

This may sound like a lot of work—it is. If you are used to turning in first drafts of your writing, then it is time to break that habit. We have seen too many groups who put numerous hours of work into their problem-solving projects but turn in a sloppy draft as their final report. Keep in mind that your credibility is enhanced or diminished by the written and spoken presentation of your work. It is essential to save enough time and effort to do this part well.

As you begin your draft, there are a number of sections that may be useful to you. They include:

- A title page
- An executive summary
- Background of the problem
- Explanation of the criteria
- Explanation of the best solution and how it meets the criteria
- Presentation of the plan
- Argued defense
- Conclusion

Title Page

You should include a title page in any professionally formatted report. A title page should include the following:

- Title
- Group name or title of task force (if appropriate)
- Members' names
- Date
- To whom the document is presented

Executive Summary

The executive summary usually contains:

- A statement of the charge
- A review of the problem-solving process

- The routing for the final report (who gets it)
- A preview of the proposal
- Acknowledgments (if appropriate)

Don't try to say too much in the executive summary. Typically, this section is 1–2 pages long. This should be a brief summary of the charge, not a rehash of what the group went through. Remember that *no one rewards you for the effort you made; you are rewarded only for the effectiveness of your final product.* Pay attention to the needs of the receiver of the report rather than justifying your own hard work. Your group is judged by the results, not by the hours spent in meetings and doing research. Make sure to spend the time necessary to articulate a report worthy of the efforts expended to find a workable solution.

The first draft that the Lawrenceville group wrote read:

> With great effort, The Planning Commission has sorted out our problem with traffic in the downtown area and presents herewith a solution to the economic deprivation that might result if the . . .

They immediately recognized the self-congratulatory tone and reworded it to be more factual:

> We were charged by the mayor to investigate complaints about traffic congestion in the downtown area. We surveyed the complaints and discovered serious impairment in the business community and tremendous inconvenience on the part of workers in plants on the margins of the borough. We set as our goal the proposal of traffic legislation to the borough council and limited ourselves to legislation requiring neither bonding nor taxation. We present this report of proposed legislation to the borough council.

You might decide to notify the reader of the nature of the proposal to be made. In our example, the LPC reported:

> Our proposal includes a plan for a community-wide carpool program designed to lighten the traffic flow.

Consider your audience carefully, though. If they are hostile to your plan, you may need to present the evidence to build the problem before you present the solution. Your group will have to decide whether to preview the solution in the executive summary of the final report.

Background

The background of the problem provides the group with an opportunity to review the case. In this section, you should include all of the evidence that a problem exists. You should include the following (with appendices as appropriate):

- Detailed description of symptoms and impairments, supported with evidence including:

- ◆ Statistics
- ◆ Scholarly research findings
- ◆ Expert and personal testimony
- ◆ Examples and illustrations
- Discussion of possible causes, supported with evidence
- Explanation of whether your group will deal with symptoms and/or causes
- Projection of what might happen if the problem is not addressed or need is not met

By the time the reader is done with this section, he/she should truly understand all the facets of the problem.

Criteria

In this section, you explain your criteria, define any terms, and explain their order of importance:

- How will the world be changed as a result of your solution?
- What criteria did you use? Define them
- Why were they important? Why were they in that order?
- Describe the specific goals you want to reach by implementing your solution.
- Discuss your limitations.

Presentation of the Plan

The proposal should be presented in complete detail. Each element of the proposal should include a statement about each of these points:

- Who? List titles of all personnel.
- Does what? Include job descriptions that are as complete as possible.
- For what reason? What does each job contribute to the solution?
- With what resources? What does each job require: equipment, specialized training, machinery, supervision, etc.?
- Under whose supervision? Show chain of command, organization chart, and communication links.
- At what cost? Budget as completely as possible. Show maximum, minimum, and most likely costs for negotiation purposes.
- To be provided by? Where is the money coming from? No sense in budgeting unless you know the cash is available.
- And evaluated as follows? Go back to your criteria and ask how you would know a successful solution when you see it.

Do not make the mistake of putting too little detail into your plan. If someone else is in charge of approving the plan, they are much more likely to do so if they can put it into immediate operation. If they have to do a lot of work to figure it out, they probably won't make the effort.

Remember that the receiver of the final report has *only* the report on which to base a judgment. An inadequate report is usually taken as a sign of an inadequate group.

Look at the difference in detail between the following two plans for implementing an honors event. Which group will have their plan implemented?

Corporate Group A

The committee believes we should have an honors celebration to be held at a date to be specified in a suitable place. A committee should be appointed to decide what awards should be given and how the winners should be selected. This recommendation should go into effect two years from now.

Corporate Group B

The committee proposes the following:

1. The heads of Sales, Marketing, Display, Transportation, Accounting, Purchasing, and Personnel should be appointed to a committee to oversee an honors celebration.

2. The committee should identify employees (no more than two in each department) who have made an outstanding contribution to the company. The "outstanding contribution" shall be a proposal or activity which has resulted in increased sales, money saved, increased efficiency, and/ or has contributed to the general welfare of employees.

3. Awards shall be an additional week's salary to be taken in cash or vacation time at the winner's discretion.

4. The purchasing agent shall buy a wall plaque on which winners can be permanently honored at a cost of no more than $5,000 and a small plaque for each winner at a cost of no more than $50. The committee shall approve the plaque design.

5. The personnel manager shall arrange an awards banquet to be held during the week between Christmas and New Year's Day at a location not more than three miles from the office and with parking accommodations for at least 300 cars. Dinner shall be served at a cost of no more than $25 per person (without drinks), and there shall be a cash bar. All personnel will be invited and may bring a guest (spouse or partner) at the expense of the company.

6. The general manager shall be responsible for supervising the operation of this report and for all publicity and notifications. The general manager shall provide a speaker for the banquet. Award speeches shall be no longer than five minutes each and acceptance speeches confined to two minutes each.

The Argued Defense

Your group must be prepared to defend its solution against whatever arguments can be raised. In most cases, persuasive proposals succeed when the proposal identifies and refutes any arguments the audience may have. In this final step, your group must deal with the question: "What can be done to prepare the most persuasive case possible for acceptance of our proposal?"

You should first assess the possible obstacles to adoption:

- Who might speak out against the proposal?
- Who stands to lose?
- Who has offered a different solution about which they might feel defensive?

Be prepared to answer the following attacks:

- There is no need/problem.
- There is a problem, but the plan is unworkable.
- There is a problem and the plan is workable, but it will not solve the problem.
- The plan is needed, workable, and will solve the problem, but it will bring undesirable effects (too costly, violates legal or moral limitations, etc.).
- The reasoning is ineffective. The documentation is ineffective.

Next, it is important to **determine what the charging authority wants**. Unfortunately, the world is not always a place where honest people do honest work and are rewarded honestly. People are often influenced by those to whom they owe favors; decision makers sometimes tend to their own interests at the expense of the organization. To make an effective appeal, you will have to look at the personal interests of those who pass judgment. Here are some issues to consider.

- The decision maker may have a sphere of influence. Does your proposal weaken or strengthen his or her influence?
- The decision maker may not be prepared to take on more work. Does your operations plan provide for additional people to reduce the pressure?
- The decision maker may be concerned about how particular individuals are affected by changes. Does your proposal displace anyone? What influence do potentially displaced people have on the decision maker? Can you protect them?

In this section of your report, you should include:

- An assessment of possible obstacles to the adoption of the solution.
- An answer to every possible argument against the solution.

- A final argument restating your solution and how it solves the problem.

Presenting the Final Report

Congratulations! You have finished the long and arduous task of completing the final report. But don't stop now. Planning the oral component is every bit as important—if not more so. It is likely that most of you have had an oral communication course. We cannot review all the skills required for effective public speaking in one chapter. Our purpose is to remind you of important general principles.

After spending extensive hours on a group project, members may be confident that they can simply "talk about" their findings. It is natural to assume that all of the information accumulated will readily spill out on demand. However, careful planning of the oral presentation is crucial to the success of the group.

Extemporaneous Speaking

A persuasive presentation requires an extemporaneous, conversational style. Keep in mind that the purpose of the oral report is to highlight the ideas in the written report. Executives do not have time to listen to you read. We witnessed one manager stop a young executive who was reading a report with the comment, "If I had wanted the report read, I would have distributed copies. Put down the manuscript and get to the point!" Extemporaneous speaking is a useful style that avoids this type of problem. It engages the audience and allows for adaptation as necessary.

Plan the Residual Message

Once you have figured out all the persuasive arguments to support your proposal, it should be easy to sum them up into a single statement expressing your purpose. We call this the residual message because it is the message that will reside in the listeners after they forget the details. Keep in mind that your purpose in speaking is not to talk, it is to have your audience remember and possibly act on your message. A well-constructed residual message will help you to achieve those goals. LPC wanted their audience to remember:

> The economic climate of our entire region depends on the implementation of a community-wide carpool program. Failure to adopt our plan for traffic control in Lawrenceville may not only mean the end of our downtown business district, it may jeopardize employment in our neighboring towns.

The commission has summarized its entire persuasive message in two sentences. Now it is relatively simple to document the assertions.

To write the residual message, complete the sentence "We want each member of our audience to agree that. . . ." Finish the sentence with a specific statement. If you avoid using the word "that," you are probably not clear enough. For example, "We want our audience to agree with our proposal" is nebulous. LPC's residual message above is much clearer. Referring to the residual message while you are designing the oral report will help to keep you focused.

Collective Planning

Once the group determines the residual message, they need to review the content of the presentation. The report loses the flavor of a group effort if only one person does the planning. As a group, you should discuss the following:

Given our residual message:

- What are the most effective arguments to use on its behalf?
- What sequence of ideas should we use?
- Who should be responsible for what?

Research Check

"Although it is generally recognized that most mainstream U.S. speeches are organized linearly, linear patterns do not represent the only logical systems available to public speakers. The organization of many Kenyan speeches could be represented as a bicycle wheel. . . . The spokes wander out repeatedly to the rim as the speaker gives an illustration, mentions a proverb, or tells a story, and then return back to the thesis at the center, though usually not exactly at the place from which they departed. Often there is only one main point in such a speech, but it is developed by an abundance of supporting material. Westerners in the audience might feel bewildered and even bored because they are unable to follow the logic that ties all the points together, whereas Kenyan listeners would be absorbed in the stories and delighted with their subtle convergence back into the central theme" (Miller, 2006, p. 243).

Putting It Together

Keep away from detailed facts and figures; use illustrations instead. Listeners, as a rule, will not remember the details of your presentation. So rather than go into the subtleties and nuances in your presentation, highlight them in the written report. The oral report should deal only with the major headings. Remember, if your oral report piques the interest of your audience, they will be curious to read the written report for more details later.

Remember too that listeners appreciate brevity. Your presentation should get to the point quickly. Twenty to forty minutes is the optimum presentation time, although there may be some occasions when a longer presentation is warranted. Many situations provide even less time. We recommend that the group verify the time limit the audience expects.

Delivering the Report

Once your group has decided on the residual message and has done the necessary documentation and outlining, you must consider the form in which the oral report should be delivered. Your group has two choices: designate a spokesperson or present the report as a group.

The most appropriate time to designate a single spokesperson is when the group does not want to appear to be "ganging up" on the administrator. In this case you can either choose your leader or your best speaker. The single spokesperson must be skilled at public speaking, understand the problem and solution completely, be able to answer questions, and be familiar with the final report.

Another option is a team presentation. If the work was divided, each member can function as an expert and cover his/her component. However, if you choose to divide the presentation, it is imperative that you know what each member is doing and that you practice together. Each section of the presentation must be sufficiently long, and the speakers adept at transitioning so that they do not appear to be jumping beans. You might create a template for each speaker to follow so that there is consistency in the presentation. Reports from groups require careful coordination of components so that the audience does not have trouble following the presentation.

Visuals

Visuals are used for a variety of reasons, including (1) helping speakers remember what they want to talk about, (2) facilitating understanding of a message, and (3) heightening listener attention and interest.

It is likely that you have been exposed to a program like PowerPoint. If not, anyone who has experience with Windows should be able to learn the program. If you don't have access to a program like this, you can generate visual aids on the computer and have them copied onto transparencies at a copy center. With the technology available today, hand-written visuals should be extinct. Whether you use an overhead, PowerPoint slide, or animated presentation, there are a few guidelines to keep in mind.

- Generally, letters must appear at least two inches tall for an audience to read them (about a 30-point font on a computer).

- If you choose color transparencies, be sure that the colors can be seen. Some cannot be distinguished from a distance. High contrast colors tend to work best.

- Don't overcrowd a visual. Typically you should never have more than 6 words per line or 6 lines per slide.

- Practice with the visual.
- Have a backup plan. We have seen computer glitches that have knocked out PowerPoint presentations. An efficient group always has a backup plan.

A sample template might look like this:

Speaker 1
Attention getter, introduction of presenters and topics
(Avoid extensive biographies, but be sure to indicate specialties and competencies.)

Speaker 2
Definition and statement of the problem
(If the question has changed from the charge, be sure to explain why.)

Speaker 3
Criteria for a solution
(Make sure legal and financial limitations are especially clear.)

Speaker 4
Explanation of discarded solutions
(Listeners need to know what was considered so they don't waste time asking.)

Speakers 5 and 6
Recommended solution
(It is not necessary to present the operations plan, but it is important to show how the solution will remedy the problem as well as to make some statement about the practicality of the solution.)

Speaker 1 returns
Summary and conclusion
(Solicit questions and direct them to appropriate group members for response.)

Practicing and Delivering the Presentation

Whether your presentation is done by an individual or a group, it will require practice. Practicing will allow your group to be sure that

- Ideas are clear, and examples make sense
- Ideas flow in a logical order
- Ideas flow from speaker to speaker
- You have met the time restrictions

This is particularly true with group presentations. Every member of your group must be competent and prepared. One hesitant and disorganized speaker can lose an audience, thereby affecting the outcome of the group's work. Group members must be honest and willing to express the limitations of members who cannot speak well. If your group has a member who lacks confidence about speaking in public, examine possible alternatives to having him or her present.

Practicing allows the group to observe and correct any distracting delivery behaviors. As you have learned in other classes, speakers should make eye contact with the audience, use correct grammar, dress appropriately, and avoid distracting mannerisms such as vocalized pauses and excessive pacing. Also, make certain that everyone in the group pays close attention to each member while he/she is speaking. It is especially distracting to the audience to watch group members confer during an oral report.

Before the actual presentation, your group should evaluate the facilities. Is all of the equipment there? Plenty of chairs? Electrical outlets? Plan for every possible item you might need. You may also want to consider the needs of your audience and supply beverages or snacks for the presentation, depending on the situation.

It is extremely important for the individual speaker or group to practice out loud before the presentation. Try to find a trial audience unfamiliar with your project. The listeners can point out what is not clear or what is distracting in the presentation.

Remember, the presentation serves as a catalyst to the report. If done well, the audience will be inspired to read the report. With all of the work that your group has put into the process so far, it is very important to keep up the energy and carefully plan and practice the final oral report. This is your chance to get the charging authority interested in your solution. If your oral report is succinct and interesting, people will want to read the final report for more detail—an essential outcome if they are to adopt your solution.

✺ Outcomes of Step Six ✺

If your group has worked hard, prepared well, and excelled in all areas, by this point, you should have a professional final report and a polished presentation. It is time to assess the outcomes. Get together as a group and decide what went well and what could have been improved. What are you most proud of and what do you wish you had done differently? Would more time really have allowed you to do better or would you have simply procrastinated longer? This debriefing session can help you make your next problem-solving experience even more successful.

✄ Member Tasks of Step Six ✄

The group members must continue to work as directed by the leader. By the time that the final decision is made, members are generally ready to be finished with the task. However, now is the time when additional motivation and expertise will put you ahead of the crowd. All of the members should participate in writing the final report—whether they plan, make graphics, proofread, or organize, each member should contribute all available skills. Members should also work to keep the motivation high while the group works on the final report.

✄ Leader Obligations of Step Six ✄

The leader needs to keep impeccable time lines and schedules as well as act to energize the group. The best way to complete the tasks of writing and presenting the final report is to follow the implementation plan line by line. The leader will need to make sure that everyone is doing what they committed to do. If a group member doesn't come through during this final phase, the entire group project and presentation can suffer. The leader is ultimately responsible and should be prepared to step in to cover for a group member who fails the group at this point.

The leader may also have to motivate the group. If members are tired or apathetic, it is important to remind them that they are almost done. Focusing on the goals, reenergizing the momentum, and keeping the end result in mind should help members to do their best.

Finally, the leader needs to let the group know what comes next. Are they finished and disbanding? Will they wait for feedback on their proposal and then continue on with revisions? Are they in charge of implementing the plan? Depending on the cohesiveness of the group, the leader may want to plan a small celebration, write thank-you notes to the members, or give each member a small gift.

FINAL THOUGHTS

A major theme in this book is that you, as a discussion participant, have many choices available to you. There are a number of practical and important roles you can play in a group. Furthermore, whatever your present level of skill, you can learn to be more effective by observing, thinking about, and understanding the discussion process. We have advocated that you leave little to chance. Group discussion is one of the best ways to display your competence to multiple audiences—from classmates to the community.

Effective discussion respects individuals and produces common goals. As an individual, you can become more productive and more satisfied by learning how to share your ideas with others, to cooperate in solving problems, and to respect the interests of individuals and groups. In a competitive world, we cannot afford to lose the contributions of intelligent and competent people. It is your responsibility to present yourself as effectively as you can by learning to be a contributing participant in group discussion. Every communication course teaches skills useful in discussion. Training in argument and debate, public speaking, rhetoric, persuasion, gender communication, interpersonal communication, nonverbal communication, and listening will prepare you for working effectively in a group.

GOALS and OUTCOMES

To prepare a final report including:

- An executive summary that contains a statement of the charge, a review of the problem-solving process, and the routing for the report
- A report on the background of the problem indicating the need for a solution
- A detailed presentation of the solution, containing (if necessary) an implementation plan, organization chart, and budget
- An argued defense of solutions, including:
  - A demonstration of how the plan will meet the need
  - A demonstration of why the plan is desirable and will bring no undesirable consequences
  - Appendices where necessary: proposals rejected with reasons for rejection, secondary plan report if one has been prepared

To prepare a final presentation including:

- A residual message that is appropriate for the audience
- A logical flow of the key ideas
- Useful and practical visuals
- A plan for who will do the speaking

MEMBER TASKS

- To work as directed by the group leader in the preparation of the final report
- To practice and participate in the presentation of the final report

LEADER OBLIGATIONS

- To see to it that the final report is written and properly transmitted
- To see to it that the group prepares and practices its final presentation of the report
- To inform the group of its disposition. Will it meet again, and when, or will it go out of business?

Bibliography

Adams, K.L., & Galanes, G. J. (2006). *Communicating in groups: Applications and skills* (6th ed.). New York: McGraw Hill.

Akiba, D., & Miller, F. (2004). The expression of cultural sensitivity in the presence of African Americans: An analysis of motives. *Small Group Research, 35*(6), 623–642.

Alavi, S., & McCormick, J. (2004). Theoretical and measurement issues for studies of collective orientation in team contexts. *Small Group Research, 35*(2), 111–127.

Allen, B. C., Sargent, L. D., & Bradley, L. M. (2003). Differential effects of task and reward interdependence on perceived helping behavior, effort, and group performance. *Small Group Research, 34*(6), 716–740.

Allen, B. J. (2002). Translating organizational communication scholarship into practice: Starting where we are. *Management Communication Quarterly, 16*(1), 101–106.

Anderson, C. M., & Martin, M. M. (1999). The relationship of argumentativeness and verbal aggressiveness to cohesion, consensus, and satisfaction in small groups. *Communication Reports, 12*(1), 21–31.

Arnold, C. C. (1974). *Criticism of oral rhetoric*. Columbus, OH: Charles E. Merrill.

Arrow, H., & Crosson, S. (2003). Musical chairs: Membership dynamics in self-organized group formation. *Small Group Research, 34*(5), 523–556.

Arrow, H., Poole, M, Henry, K., Wheelan, S., & Moreland, R. (2004). Time, change, and development: The temporal perspective on groups. *Small Group Research, 35*(1), 73–105.

Aubert, B., & Kelsey, B. (2003). Further understanding of trust and performance in virtual teams. *Small Group Research, 34*(5), 575–618.

Bargal, D. (2004). Structure and process in reconciliation transformation workshops: Encounters between Israeli and Palestinian youth. *Small Group Research, 35*(5), 596–616.

Bayazit, M., & Mannix, E. A. (2003). Should I stay or should I go? *Small Group Research, 34*(3), 290–321.

Bayless, O. L. (1967). An alternate pattern for problem solving discussion. *The Journal of Communication, 17*, 188–197.

Beatty, M. J. (1988). Increasing students' choice-making consistency: The effect of decision-rule-use training. *Communication Education, 37*, 95–105.

Beebe, S. A., & Masterson, J. T. (2006). *Communicating in small groups: Principles and practices* (8th ed.). Boston: Allyn & Bacon.

Berg, D. M. (1967). A thematic approach to the analysis of the task-oriented, small group. *The Central States Speech Journal, 18*, 285–291.

Beauchamp, M. R., Bray, S. R., Eys, M. A., & Carron, A. B. (2005). Leadership behaviors and multidemensional role ambiguity perceptions in team sports. *Small Group Research, 36*(1), 5–20.

Bonito, J. A., & Lambert, B. L. (2005). Information similarity as a moderator of the effect of gender on participation in small groups: A multi-level analysis. *Small Group Research, 36*(2), 139–165.

Borchers, G. L. (1968). John Dewey and speech education. *Western Speech, 32*, 127–137.

Bordia, P., Defonzo, N., & Chang, A. (1999). Rumor as group problem solving. *Small Group Research, 30*(1), 8–28.

Bormann, E. G. (1994). Response to "revitalizing the study of small group communication." *Communication Studies, 45*, 86–91.

Bormann, E. G., & Bormann, N. G. (1996). *Effective small group communication* (6th ed.). Minneapolis: Burgess International.

Bradley, J., White, B. J., & Mennecke, B. E. (2003). Teams and tasks. *Small Group Research, 34*(3), 353–387.

Bray, S. R. (2004). Collective efficacy, group goals, and group performance of a muscular endurance task. *Small Group Research, 35*(2), 230–238.

Bray, S. R., Brawley, L. R., & Carron, A. V. (2002). Efficacy for interdependent role functions. *Small Group Research, 33*(6), 644–666.

Brilhart, J. K. (1966). An experimental comparison of three techniques for communicating a problem-solving pattern to members of a discussion group. *Speech Monographs, 33*, 168–177.

Brilhart, J. K., & Jochem, L. M. (1964). Effects of different patterns on outcomes of problem-solving discussion. *Journal of Applied Psychology, 48*, 175–179.

Butler D., & Geis, F. L. (1990). Nonverbal affect responses to male and female leaders. Implications for leadership evaluations. *Journal of Personality and Social Psychology, 58*, 48–59.

Caldwell, D. F., & O'Reilly, C. A., III. (2003). The determinants of team-based innovation in organizations. *Small Group Research, 34*(4), 497–517.

Carron, A., Brawley, L., Bray, S., Eys, M., Dorsch, K., Estabrooks, P., et al. (2004). Using consensus as a criterion for groupness: implications for the cohesion-group success relationship. *Small Group Research, 35*(4), 466–491.

Carron, A., Brawley, L., Eys, M., Bray, S., Dorsch, K., Estabrooks, P., et al. (2003). Do individual perceptions of group cohesion reflect shared beliefs? *Small Group Research, 34*(4), 468–496.

Cathcart, R. S., Samovar, L. A., & Henman, L. (1995). *Small group communication: A reader* (7th ed.). New York: McGraw Hill.

Chansler, P. A., Swamidass, P. M., & Cammann, C. (2003). Self-managing work teams: An empirical study of group cohesiveness in 'natural work groups' at a Harley-Davidson Motor Company plant. *Small Group Research, 34*(1), 101–120.

Chirumbolo, A., Mannetti, L., Pierro, A., Areni, A., & Kruglanski, A. (2005). Motivated closed-mindedness and creativity in small groups. *Small Group Research, 36*(1), 59–82.

Cline, R. J. W. (1990). Detecting groupthink: Methods for observing the illusion of unanimity. *Communication Quarterly, 38,* 112–126.

Crowell, L. (1953). Criteria are critical. *Western Speech, 17,* 245–248.

Dahlback, O. (2003). A conflict theory of group risk taking. *Small Group Research, 34*(3), 251–289.

Daniels, M. (2002). Teaching small group communication using first class software. *Qualitative Research Reports in Communication, 3*(2), 32–38.

Dewey, J. (1910). *How we think.* New York: D. C. Heath.

Dewey, J. (1933). *How we think: A restatement of the relation of reflective thinking to the educative process* (2nd ed.). Boston: D. C. Heath.

Droge, D. (2004). Book review of *Small group communication: Theory and practice* (8th ed.). *Communication Education, 53*(4), 365–372.

Duffy, D. (1999, January 15). Cultural evolution. *CIO Enterprise Magazine.* Retrieved May 24, 2006, from http://www.cio.com/archive/enterprise/011599_rah_content.html

Ehniger, D. (1943). A logic of discussion method. *Quarterly Journal of Speech, 29,* 163–168.

Ellis, D. G., & Fisher, B. A. (1994). *Small group decision making* (4th ed.). New York: McGraw Hill.

Engleberg, I. N., & Wynn, D. R. (2003). *Working in groups: Communication principles and strategies* (3rd ed.). New York: Houghton Mifflin.

English, A., Griffith, R. L., & Steelman, L. A. (2004). Team performance: The effect of team conscientiousness and task type. *Small Group Research, 35*(6), 643–665.

Erbert, L. A., Mearns, G. M., & Dena, S. (2005). Perceptions of turning points and dialectical interpretations in organizational team development. *Small Group Research, 36*(1), 21–58.

Fisher, B. A., & Beach, W. A. (1979). Content and relationship dimensions of communicative behavior: An exploratory study. *Western Journal of Speech Communication, 43,* 201–211.

Fisher, B. A., & Ellis, D. G. (1990). *Small group decision making: Communication and the group process* (3rd ed.). New York: McGraw Hill.

Flippen, A. R. (April, 1999). Understanding groupthink from a self-regulatory perspective. *Small Group Research, 30*(2), 139–165.

Foels, R., Driskell, J. E., Mullen, B., & Salas, E. (December, 2000). The effects of democratic leadership on group member satisfaction: An integration. *Small Group Research, 31*(6), 676–701.

Frey, L. R. (1994). Introduction: Revitalizing the study of small group communication. *Communication Studies, 45,* 1–6.

Frey, L. R., & Barge, J. K. (Eds.). (1997). *Managing group life: Communication in decision-making groups.* New York: Houghton Mifflin.

Frey, L. R., & Wolf, S. (2004). The symbolic-interpretive perspective on group dynamics. *Small Group Research, 35*(3), 277–306.

Galanes, G. (2003, December 1). In their own words: An exploratory study of bona fide group leaders. *Small Group Research, 34*(6), 741–770.

Galanes, G. J., & Adams, K. (2007). *Effective group discussion* (12th ed.). New York: McGraw Hill.

Gastil, J., & Dillard, J. P. (1999). Increasing political sophistication through public deliberation. *Political Communication, 16*(1), 3–23.

Gershenoff, A. B., & Foti, R. J. (2003). Leader emergence and gender roles in all-female groups. *Small Group Research, 34*(2), 170–196.

Gibson, C. B. (2003). Quality of team service. *Small Group Research, 34*(5), 619–646.

Gibson, C. B., & Saxton, T. (2005). Thinking outside the black box: Outcomes of team decisions with third-party intervention. *Small Group Research, 36*(2), 208–236.

Gouran, D. S. (1990). Evaluating group outcomes. In G. M. Phillips (Ed.), *Teaching how to work in groups* (pp. 175–196). Norwood, NJ: Ablex.

Gouran, D. S. (1991). Rational approaches to decision-making and problem-solving discussion. *Quarterly Journal of Speech, 77,* 343–358.

Gouran, D. S. (2003, Spring). Reflections on the type of question as a determinant of the form of interaction in decision-making and problem-solving discussions. *Communication Quarterly, 51*(2), 111–126.

Gouran, D. S., & Hirokawa, R. Y. (1986). Counteractive functions of communication in effective group decision-making. In R. Y. Hirokawa & M. S. Poole (Eds.), *Communication and group decision-making* (pp. 81–90). Beverly Hills, CA: Sage.

Graham, C. R. (2003). A model of norm development for computer-mediated teamwork. *Small Group Research, 34*(3), 322–352.

Grosse, C. U. (2002, December). Managing communication within virtual intercultural teams. *Business Communication Quarterly, 65*(4), 22–39.

Halfhill, T., Sundstrom, E., Lahner, J., Calderone, W., & Nielsen, T. M. (2005). Group personality composition and group effectiveness: An integrative review of empirical research. *Small Group Research, 36*(1), 83–105.

Halverson, S. K., Murphy, S. E., & Riggio, R. E. (2004). Charismatic leadership in crisis situations: A laboratory investigation of stress and crisis. *Small Group Research, 35*(5), 495–514.

Hardy, J., Eys, M., & Carron, A. (2005). Exploring the potential disadvantages of high cohesion in sports teams. *Small Group Research, 36*(2), 166–187.

Hare, A. P. (2003). Roles, relationships, and groups in organizations: Some conclusions and recommendations. *Small Group Research, 34*(2), 123–154.

Harper, N. L., & Askling, L. (1980). Group communication and quality of task solution in a media production organization, *Communication Monographs, 47,* 77–100.

Hart, R. P., & Burks, D. (1972). Rhetorical sensitivity and social interaction. *Speech Monographs, 24,* 75–91.

Henningsen, D., & Henningsen, M. (2003). Examining social influence in information-sharing contexts. *Small Group Research, 34*(4), 391–412.

Henningsen, D., Henningsen, M., Eden, J., & Cruz, M. G. (2006, February). Examining the symptoms of groupthink and retrospective sensemaking. *Small Group Research, 37*(1), 36–64.

Hirokawa, R. Y. (1980). A comparative analysis of communication patterns within effective and ineffective decision-making groups. *Communication Monographs, 47,* 312–321.

Hirokawa, R. Y. (1983). Group communication and problem-solving effectiveness: An investigation of group phases. *Human Communication Research, 9,* 291–305.

Hirokawa, R. Y. (1988). Group communication research: Considerations for the use of interaction analysis. In C. H. Tardy (Ed.), *A handbook for the study of human communication: Methods and instruments for observing, measuring, and assessing communication processes* (pp. 229–245). Norwood, NJ: Ablex.

Hirokawa, R. Y., & Pace, R. C. (1983). A descriptive investigation of the possible communication-based reasons for effective and ineffective group decision making. *Communication Monographs, 50*, 363–379.

Hobman, E., Bordia, P., Irmer, B., & Chang, A. (2002, August 1). The expression of conflict in computer-mediated and face-to-face groups. *Small Group Research, 33*(4), 439–465.

Hoegl, M., & Parboteeah, K. P. (2003). Goal setting and team performance in innovative projects: On the moderating role of teamwork quality. *Small Group Research, 34*(1), 3–19.

Hogg, M. A., Abrams, D., Otten, S., & Hinkle, S. (2004). The social identity perspective: Intergroup relations, self-conception, and small groups. *Small Group Research, 35*(3), 246–276.

Hollingshead, A. B., & Poole, M. S. (2004). Interdisciplinary theoretical perspectives of small groups Part II. *Small Group Research, 35*(3), 243–245.

Janis, I. L. (1972). *Victims of groupthink.* Boston: Houghton Mifflin.

Johnson, S. D., & Iacobucci, C. (1995). Teaching small group communication with the dream team. *Communication Education, 44*(2), 177–183.

Jurma, W. E. (1979). Effects of leader structuring style and task orientation characteristics on group members. *Communication Monographs, 46*, 282–295.

Karakowsky, L., McBey, K., & Miller, D. L. (2004). Gender, perceived competence, and power displays: Examining verbal interruptions in a group context. *Small Group Research, 35*(4), 407–439.

Katz, N., Lazer, D., Arrow, H., & Contractor, N. (2004). Network theory and small groups. *Small Group Research, 35*(3), 307–332.

Keyton, J. (2006). Communicating in groups: Developing relationships for group effectiveness (3rd ed.). New York: Oxford.

Kilmann, R. H., & Thomas, K. W. (1977). Developing a forced-choice measure of conflict-handling behavior: The MODE instrument. *Educational and Psychological Measurements, 37*, 309–325.

Koch, S. C. (2005). Evaluative affect display toward male and female leaders of task oriented groups. *Small Group Research, 36*(6), 678–703.

Lammers, J. C., & Krikorian, D. H. (1997). Theoretical extension and operationalization of the bona fide group construct with an application to surgical teams. *Journal of Applied Communication Research, 25*(1), 17–39.

Larson, C. E. (1969). Forms of analysis and small group problem-solving. *Speech Monographs, 36*, 452–455.

LaRusso, D. A., & Tucker, R. K. (1957). Discussion outlines and skill in reflective thinking. *The Speech Teacher, 6*, 139–142.

Lindsley, S. L., & Braithwaite, C. A. (2006). U.S. Americans and Mexicans working together: Five core concepts. In L. A. Samovar, R. E. Porter, & E. R. McDaniel (Eds.), *Intercultural communication: A reader* (pp. 280–286). Belmont, CA: Thompson/Wadsworth.

Lodewljkx, H. F. M., van Zomeren, M., & Syroit, J. E. M. M. (2005). The anticipation of a severe initiation: Gender differences in effects on affiliation tendency and group attraction. *Small Group Research, 36*(2), 237–262.

Mason, C. M., & Griffin, M. A. (2003). Identifying group task satisfaction at work. *Small Group Research, 34*(4), 413–442.

McBurney, J. H., & Hance, K. G. (1939). *Principles and methods of discussion.* New York: Harper.

McBurney, J. H., & Hance, K. G. (1933, 1950). *Discussion in human affairs*. New York: Harper.

McLeod, P. L., & Kettner-Polley, R. B. (2004). Contributions of psychodynamic theories to understanding small groups. *Small Group Research, 35*(3), 333–361.

Meyers, R. A., & Brashers, D. E. (1994). Expanding the boundaries of small group communication research: Exploring a feminist perspective. *Communication Studies, 45*, 68–85.

Miller, A. N. (2006). Public speaking patterns in Kenya. In L. A. Samovar, R. E. Porter, & E. R. McDaniel (Eds.), *Intercultural communication: A reader* (pp. 238–245). Belmont, CA: Thompson/Wadsworth.

Miura, A., & Hida, M. (2004). Synergy between diversity and similarity in group-idea generation. *Small Group Research, 35*(5), 540–564.

Mohammed, S., & Angell, L. C. (2003). Personality heterogeneity in teams: Which differences make a difference for team performance? *Small Group Research, 34*(6), 651–677.

Molleman, E., Mauta, A., & Jehn, K. A. (2004). Person-job fit applied to team-work: A multilevel approach. *Small Group Research, 35*(5), 515–539.

Olivera, F., & Stras, S. G. (2004). Group-to-individual transfer of learning: Cognitive and social factors. *Small Group Research, 35*(4), 440–465.

Paletz, S. B. F., Peng, K., Erez, M., & Maslach, C. (2004). Ethnic composition and its differential impact on group processes in diverse teams. *Small Group Research, 35*(2), 128–157.

Pan, P. J. D., & Lin, C. W. (2004). Members' perceptions of leader behaviors, group experiences, and therapeutic factors in group counseling. *Small Group Research, 35*(2), 174–194.

Pavitt, C. (1993). Does communication matter in social influence during small group discussion? Five positions. *Communication Studies, 44*, 216–227.

Pescosolido, A. T. (2003). Group efficacy and group effectiveness: The effects of group efficacy over time on group performance and development. *Small Group Research, 34*(1), 20–42.

Phillips, G. M. (1965). PERT as a logical adjunct to the discussion process. *Journal of Communication, 15*, 89–99.

Phillips, G. M. (1966). *Communication and the small group*. Indianapolis: Bobbs-Merrill.

Poole, M. S. (1981). Decision development in small groups I: A comparison of two models. *Communication Monographs, 48*, 1–24.

Poole, M. S. (1990). Do we have any theories of group communication? *Communication Studies, 41*, 237–247.

Poole, M. S., Hollingshead, A. B., McGrath, J. E., Moreland, R. L., & Rohrbaugh, J. (2004). Interdisciplinary perspectives on small groups. *Small Group Research, 35*(1), 3–16.

Poole, M. S., Holmes, M., Watson, R., & DeSanctis, G. (1993). Group decision support systems and group communication: A comparison of decision making in computer-supported and nonsupported groups. *Communication Research, 20*, 176–213.

Priola, V., Smith, J. L., & Armstrong, S. J. (2004). Group work and cognitive style. *Small Group Research, 35*(5), 565–595.

Propp, K. M., & Nelson, D. (1996). Problem-solving performance in naturalistic groups: A test of the ecological validity of the functional perspective. *Communication Studies, 47*(1-2), 35–46.

Propp, K. M., & Kreps, G. L. (1994). A rose by any other name: The vitality of group communication research. *Communication Studies, 45*, 7–19.

Putnam, L. L. (1994). Revitalizing small group communication: Lessons learned from a bona fide group perceptive. *Communication Studies, 45*, 97–102.

Pyron, H. C. (1964). An experimental study of the role of reflective thinking in business and professional conferences and discussions. *Speech Monographs, 31*, 157–161.

Pyron, H. C., & Sharp, H., Jr. (1963). A quantitative study of reflective thinking and performance in problem-solving discussion. *The Journal of Communication, 13*, 46–53.

Riddle, B. L., Anderson, C. M., & Martin, M. M. (2000) Small group socialization scale. *Small Group Research, 31*(5), 554–572.

Rothwell, J. D. (2007). *In mixed company: Small group communication* (6th ed.). Belmont, CA: Thompson/Wadsworth.

Roy, M. H. (2001). Small group communication and performance: Do cognitive flexibility and context matter? *Management Decision, 39*(4), 323–330.

Rozell, E. J., & Gundersen, D. E. (2003). The effects of leader impression management on group perceptions of cohesion, consensus, and communication. *Small Group Research, 34*(2), 197–222.

Salanova, M., Llorens, S., Cifre, E., Martinez, I. M., & Schaufeli, W. B. (2003). Perceived collective efficacy subjective well-being and task performance among electronic work groups: An experimental study. *Small Group Research, 34*(1), 43–73.

Sanders, K., & Naute, A. (2004). Social cohesiveness and absenteeism: The relationship between characteristics of employees and short-term absenteeism within an organization. *Small Group Research, 35*(6), 724–741.

Scheidel, T. M., & Crowell, L. (1979). *Discussing and deciding: A desk book*. New York: Macmillan.

Schultz, B. G. (1996). *Communicating in the small group: Theory and practice* (2nd ed.). White Plains, NY: Longman Books.

Schultz, B., Ketrow, S., & Urban, D. (1995, November). Improving decision quality in the small group: The role of the reminder. *Small Group Research, 26*(4), 521–541.

Seibold, D. R. (1994). More reflection or more research? To (re)vitalize small group communication research, let's "just do it." *Communication Studies, 45*, 103–110.

Sell, J., Lovaglia, M. J., Mannix, E. A., Samuelson, C. D., & Wilson, R. K. (2004). Investigating conflict, power, and status within and among groups. *Small Group Research, 35*(1), 44–72.

Seyfarth, B. (2000). Structuration theory in small group communication: A review and agenda for future research. *Communication Yearbook, 23*, 341.

Sharp, H., Jr., & Milliken, J. (1964). Reflective thinking ability and the product of problem-solving discussion. *Speech Monographs, 31*, 124–127.

Sinclair, A. L. (2003). The effects of justice and cooperation on team effectiveness. *Small Group Research, 34*(1), 74–100.

Smith, M. J. (1988). *Contemporary communication research methods*. Belmont, CA: Wadsworth.

Strijbos, J.-W., Martens, R. L., Jochems, W. M. G., & Broers, N. J. (2004). The effect of functional roles on group efficiency: Using multilevel modeling and content analysis to investigate computer-supported collaboration in small groups. *Small Group Research, 35*(2), 195–229.

Sturgis, A. (2001). The standard code of parliamentary procedure (4th ed.). New York: McGraw-Hill.

Tagger, S., & Brown, T. C. (2006, February). Interpersonal affect and peer rating bias in teams. *Small Group Research, 37*(1), 86–111.

Topi, H., Valacich, J. S., & Rao, M. T. (2002). The effects of personality and media differences on the performance of dyads addressing a cognitive conflict task. *Small Group Research, 33*(6), 667–701.

Tschan, F. (2002). Ideal cycles of communication (or cognitions) in triads, dyads, and individuals. *Small Group Research, 33*(6), 615–643.

Tubbs, S. L. (1997). *Systems approach to small group interaction* (6th ed.). New York: McGraw Hill.

Van Emmerick, I. H., Lambooy, M., & Sanders, K. (2002). Differential effects of individual-linked and team-level status allocation on professionals' job performance. *Small Group Research, 33*(6), 702–717.

Van Hiel, A., & Franssen, V. (2003). Information acquisition bias during the preparation of group discussion: A comparison of prospective minority and majority members. *Small Group Research, 34*(5), 557–574.

Vanderloot, L. (2002). Functional and causal explanations in group communication research. *Communication Theory, 12*(4), 469–486.

Von Bertelanffy, L. (1968). *General systems theory*. New York: Braziller.

Wagner, R. H., & Arnold, C. C. (1950). *Handbook of group discussion*. Boston: Houghton Mifflin.

Wall, V. D., Jr., & Galanes, G. J. (1986). The SYMLOG dimensions and small group conflict. *Central States Speech Journal, 37*, 61–78.

Weinberg, H. (1959). *Levels of knowing and existence*. New York: Harper.

Wheelan, S. A., Davidson, B., & Tilin, F. (2003). Group development across time. *Small Group Research, 34*(2), 223–245.

Wheelan, S. A., & Williams, T. (2003). Mapping dynamic interaction patterns in work groups. *Small Group Research, 34*(4), 443–467.

Whiteoak, J. W., Chalip, L., & Hort, L. K. (2004). Assessing group efficacy: Comparing three methods of measurement. *Small Group Research, 35*(2), 158–173.

Wilmot, W. W., & Hocker, J. L. (2007). *Interpersonal conflict* (7th ed.). New York: McGraw Hill.

Wilson, G. L. (1998). *Groups in context* (5th ed.). New York: McGraw Hill.

Wittenbaum, G. M., Hollingshead, A. B., Paulus, P. B., Hirokawa, R. Y., Ancona, D. G., Peterson, R. S. et al. (2004). The functional perspective as a lens for understanding groups. *Small Group Research, 35*(1), 17–43.

Wood, J. T. (1977a). Constructive climate in discussion: Learning to manage disagreements effectively. In J. W. Pfeiffer & J. E. Jones (Eds.), *1977 group facilitators' annual handbook*. La Jolla, CA: University Associates.

Wood, J. T. (1977b). Leading in purposive discussions: A study of adaptive behavior. *Communication Monographs, 44*, 152–165.

Wood, J. T. (2007). *Gendered lives: Communication, gender, and culture* (7th ed.). Belmont, CA: Wadsworth.

Yamaguchi, R., & Maehr, M. L. (2004). Children's emergent leadership: The relationships with group characteristics and outcomes. *Small Group Research, 35*(4), 388–406.

Zornoza, A., Ripoll, P., & Peiró, J. M. (2002). Conflict management in groups that work in two different communication contexts: Face-to-face and computer-mediated communication. *Small Group Research, 3*(5), 481–508.

✑ Index ✑

175